Little Paul tackles big Paul

SOCCER SKILLS WITH

GAZZA

PAUL GASCOIGNE AND MEL STEIN

ILLUSTRATIONS BY PAUL TREVILLION

STANLEY PAUL

LONDON SYDNEY AUCKLAND JOHANNESBURG

To my Mum and Dad

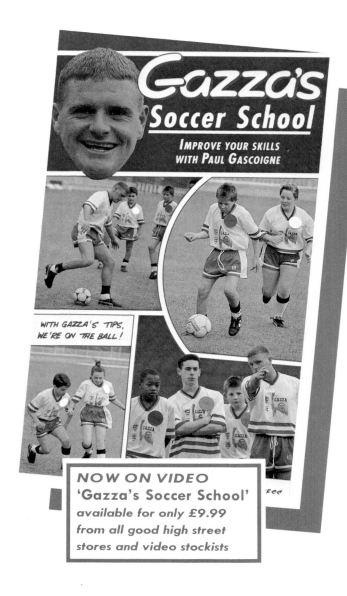

First published 1991

Reprinted in 1993

© Paul Gascoigne Promotions 1991

Paul Gascoigne & Mel Stein have asserted their
right under the Copyright, Designs and Patents
Act, 1988 to be identified as the authors of
this work

First published in the United Kingdom in 1991 by
Stanley Paul & Co. Limited
Random House, 20 Vauxhall Bridge Road,
London SW1V 2SA

Random House Australia (Pty) Limited
20 Alfred Street, Milsons Point, Sydney
New South Wales 2061, Australia

Random House New Zealand Limited
18 Poland Road, Glenfield
Auckland 10, New Zealand

Random House South Africa (Pty) Limited
PO Box 337, Bergvlei, South Africa

Random House UK Limited Reg. No. 954009

A CIP catalogue record for this book
is available from the British Library

ISBN 0 09 178147 7

Printed and bound in Great Britain by
Butler & Tanner Ltd, Frome and London

CONTENTS

Acknowledgements

I'd like to thank everybody who helped me with this book. In particular, Paul Trevillion, whose brilliant illustrations make it so much easier to understand; David Cannon, whose photographs show what an exciting game football can be (and even manage to make me look quite pretty!); Colin Suggett whose invaluable coaching of me as a kid made so much possible and who helped me pass it on to the kids who worked with me at Wembley; Glen Roeder, for showing me the famous shuffle and getting me to the church on time; everybody at Chrysalis and Channel 4, but particularly Neil Duncanson who aged visibly from the minute I met him; all the kids who played at Wembley but a special thank you to the two fine young goalkeepers Andrew Quy and Paul Sheridan; to Puma, Stuart Surridge and Aitch for supplying the kit, Wembley Stadium for supplying the stadium, all the schools for supplying the children (particularly City of London who provided three of them); John Brewer of the Football Association National Human Performance Centre at Lilleshall Hall who provided the diet, promptly, beautifully typed and free of charge; Jayne Ball, who typed the book, then re-typed it, then typed it again (thank goodness for word processors); and finally Mel Stein, who this time didn't catch a cold on a fishing boat but settled for influenza at Wembley!

Match action photographs by courtesy of AllSport, Colorsport and Bob Thomas

My guru Mel Stein (right) and my illustrator Paul Trevillion (alias D. J. Bear) try to pick up a trick or two from watching yours truly

INTRODUCTION

*I*t was Kevin Keegan who said, 'In football, you have to compete.' When somebody as influential in the game as Kevin says anything you have to listen.

For me, football is the most important thing in my life, it's what I feel I was put on this earth for, to play, to entertain, to listen, to learn and to pass on what I've learned to people like you. I don't know you individually, but if you've bought, borrowed or stolen this book then I know something about you. I know you can read (or at least look at the pictures), I know you've heard of me, Gazza, I know you play football and I know you want to get better at playing.

Not all of you can play for England, not all of you will get the chance to be paid for playing football, not all of you will even make the first team at your schools and clubs – but that shouldn't stop you wanting to be the best at whatever level you play, it shouldn't stop you wanting to be a winner. Me, Gazza, I hate losing. I make no bones about it, because if I've lost, if my team's lost, then I have to examine my game to see what I did wrong. Even if my ten team mates had a nightmare, and the papers said I was brilliant (which has only happened in my dreams) I'd still have to re-examine my part in the defeat, to replay every pass, every move, to retake every corner, just to see where I could have done better.

I'm still young, I'm still learning and I suspect that most of the readers of this book will be even younger than me. I've a long way to go in the game but I reckon that makes me better qualified to write a book of this kind. I've not given up playing twenty years ago; I don't think I know everything; it's all new to me as well as to you, and while it's fresh in my mind I aim to pass it on.

Sometimes I'm accused of not taking the game seriously enough. Those who say that have to be joking themselves. I'm not saying you have to cry when things go wrong, nor am I in any way suggesting that moaning and groaning to the referee can ever be right or justified – but you have to care enough to want to cry and complain – and then you have to be strong enough not to. As I say, I'm still working at that part of the game myself and I've little doubt that I'll get it wrong sometimes in my future career. The thing to do, though, is to learn from your mistakes and get it right the next time.

I don't think I touched that German player when I was booked in the semi-final of the World Cup, but you can be sure that if I ever play in a match like that again I'll think twice before committing myself to the sort of tackle which gives the player a chance of taking a dive, or the referee a chance of making a mistake. That's what I mean by learning all the time.

I hope this book will make you realise that football is not just kicking a ball about and hoping it goes in the right direction. It's a science, an art form, a subject to study just like maths, chemistry or history. Maybe, like me, you're not brilliant at school work, maybe you've more skill in your feet than your head – that's nothing to be ashamed of. You have to work at that skill and develop it, just like the kid who lives next door works at his English homework, just like the kid who can paint works at his easel.

You have to care, you have to want to win, but you have to enjoy doing it, and I hope that this book will bring you hours of enjoyment, and that at the end of it you will be a much better footballer. We can't all be winners but we can all be triers, we can all be competitors. Go out there and compete!

MENTAL PREPARATION AND APPLICATION •1

You can't just wake up on the morning of a match and think, 'Oh, well, ninety minutes and then I'm off out.' Each game has to be approached as if it's the Cup Final, as if it's the only game of the season. You often hear managers saying, 'We're going to treat this match as a cup tie,' but for me – and for you – every match has to be a cup tie. If you lose you can't have the game played over again, and losing points should mean as much to you as going out of a competition.

It's no coincidence that my professional advisers and Tottenham have agreed that for two clear days before any match I take on no commercial activities. If a game is on a Saturday, although I'm thinking about it from the minute I get off the pitch the previous Saturday, it's from Thursday on that I really start to get psyched up. Yet you can't go over the top. In the televised game against Liverpool in the 1990/91 season when Spurs lost 3–1, I think I was too tense before the match. It's no good going on to the pitch wound up tight, you have to strike a happy balance.

So, before the match, this is what you have to do:

1 Make sure you're perfectly fit. You can't ride a bike with a puncture and you can't play football to the best of your ability with an injury.

2 Think about who you're playing. If you've played them before, try and remember the mistakes they made – and the errors you committed. Pick out their best players and don't get frightened by them. If you go on to the pitch afraid, it's like starting 0–1 down. However, don't underestimate your opponents. If they've one or two class players then you may need to mark them man to man. Always be prepared to change your tactics according to who you're playing. Two great managers in the First Division are Kenny Dalglish and Terry Venables and it's no coincidence that they're also great tacticians. How many managers would have the courage to leave players of the talent of Peter Beardsley and Paul Walsh on the bench for tactical reasons?

3 Relax ... but not too much. Get yourself hyped up before the match, but in the dressing room try to relax. I often feel sick before a match. It's not unnatural. Players who've made 500 appearances still disappear, white-faced and shaking, into the toilets, just before it's time to get onto the pitch. Just sit quietly, take deep breaths, then breathe evenly and regularly. Close your eyes. Ignore what's going on around you. Imagine you're on your own. It's just you and the opposition. Close everything else out of your mind – it's a bit like hypnotising yourself, a bit like getting your balance on a tightrope. It's only when you're perfectly balanced that you should take the next step and it's only when you're perfectly ready that you should go on to the pitch.

And during the match you should:

1 Concentrate on the match. You can't perform to your best if you're thinking of something else. Your latest girlfriend will have to wait until after the match. Sometimes you see players caught out, either at the back when the striker raced by them, or up front when they simply don't seem to be expecting the ball. Always expect the ball. Nine times out of ten you'll be disappointed, you may do a lot of calling and running for nothing, but at the end of the day at least your mind won't wander.

2 Ignore the crowd. Sometimes when there's only a dozen people watching a school match it can be worse than 100,000 packed into an international stadium. If there's only a few people, you can hear every word they say and quite often what they say doesn't make any sense. I've seen kids, and I've seen professionals, panic when instructions or criticism are yelled at them from the bench. I'm a great believer in sticking to the rule that says no coaching from the touchline. It can't help, it can only confuse. Provided you're putting into practice what you've been doing in training, then you're doing your best, and people shouting at you isn't going to make it any better. Try and block out all sounds, or try and make them just merge into one enormous roar, which is just for you, just urging *you* on. Ignore any abuse the crowd throws at you. It is intended to get to you, to put you off your game. Don't play into their hands. I remember one young black player who while playing away was so badly abused by the home crowd that his game went to pieces and the manager had to take him off at half time. He's since moved down a division or two and is just rebuilding his career. Racial taunts are even worse than anything else (and believe me I've had my fill of everything else!); you just have to close your ears and your mind to it and get on with the game.

3 If you make a mistake, forget it (for the moment). We all make mistakes. Fortunately, football's not like cricket. If you misread a ball at cricket you get bowled, that's it. You're back in the pavilion until the second innings. In a game of football, particularly at the pace we play the game in England, you're bound to make mistakes. What you have to make sure of is that no one mistake stops you concentrating on the rest of the game. Quite how I carried on in that World Cup semi-final I'll never know, but looking at the video of what happened after I got booked makes interesting and educational viewing. Gary Lineker, Chris Waddle, Terry Butcher, all in their own way played a part in calming me down. I then realised the match was there for winning, and whether or not I could play in the Final was irrelevant. I had to get on with the game, and in fact some of my most telling and effective tackles and passes were made after the booking. Even if you score an own goal, forget it. Just try harder. It's amazing how many times a player scores at both ends – that can't just be coincidence.

4 Be a team member. Whatever you do off the pitch always remember that you're part of a team on it. Be aware of your team mates, not just as players, but as individuals. Understand their strengths and their weaknesses. Help them through the game and they'll help you. I'm often accused of being greedy, of trying to do too much myself. I think that in my younger days that was a fair accusation, but now I do try and pass whenever possible. However, if I see a path to a goal that's clearer for me than any of my team mates, I go down it. Sometimes it works, sometimes it doesn't. When it does I'm a hero, when it doesn't I'm a greedy so-and-so; but I never set out on a run intending to be greedy. If I do it, it's because I think it's best for the team at that particular moment.

5 Obey the referee. 'Oh yes,' I hear you say, 'why doesn't he practise what he preaches?' Believe me, I really do try. I won't go into what happened against Manchester United in January 1991 but I've made myself a private promise that

even if a referee asks for my telephone number with a view to taking me out to dinner I'm not going to give it to him. This book is about principles. Obviously neither you nor I can put into practice these principles for ninety minutes of every match; but we have to lay down standards for ourselves. If we fall short of those standards then we're open to be criticised by ourselves, by the manager, by our team mates, or in my case by the media. We have to accept that (a) the referee is right even when he's wrong and (b) he's more likely to book you than change his decision if you argue with him. Remember those two golden rules and try to treat the referee as a friend. He's there to guide you and the other twenty-one players through the game; provided you behave yourself he's there to protect you. Don't treat the ref as an enemy – he may not be on your side, but he's not on the other side either.

Even when the game's over you can still learn; here's what to do after the match:

1 Listen to criticism and advice. Post-match analysis can be heated or it can be calm. Throwing your boots into the corner of the dressing room and storming off into the showers doesn't do anybody any good. Sometimes the most constructive criticism of your game can be made immediately after it. By the time Monday comes around and it's reduced to drawings and diagrams, your mistakes can be old news, something you'd rather forget than replay. Be prepared to listen, not only to your manager, but also to your team mates. Sometimes words said in anger might be hurtful but they can also be truthful, and often your team mates are the best people to tell you about your mistakes.

2 Analyse your own game. Use the week between matches not just to look ahead but to look back. Think about your mistakes now, think about the criticism you've received, be honest with yourself over the weaknesses in your game, and work on them. Obviously you should practise your skills but if you just practise what you're good at then you're fooling yourself. It's great in practice to do the things you can do, it can be boring and depressing to work on the things you can't do – but if you work on them, then the things you can't do become the things you can do – if you see what I mean. A lot of football's in the mind. If your mind's not clear then the muddle will go all the way down to your feet – and you can't play football with muddled feet, can you?

2 · DIET

No, this chapter's not a joke. What is a joke was the diet I used to live on. Now I realise that sweets, pop, ice cream, burgers – they're all fine for kids, they're OK if you want an occasional treat, but a trained athlete needs something different, he needs a well-balanced consistent diet that not only does him good but makes him feel good. Everybody has to arrive at what's right for them by themselves. What I've done below is just to set out some suggestions which you might want to try. However, if you're in any doubt at all about what you should or shouldn't eat before or after a match then ask your doctor or a trained dietician. Whatever you do don't make yourself ill – it's just not worth it.

First of all find out what's the correct weight for your height and build. Some people are naturally big-boned and weigh more than others of the same height, so even that's not necessarily an acid test. Weigh yourself every day, it's much better to keep day-to-day control than to have a big splurge on your weight with a crash diet.

Second, remember you are what you eat. If you eat rubbish you become rubbish, if you eat healthy you are healthy. So here's a typical Gazza menu for a day:

Breakfast:
  Orange juice. (If it's cold get a hot drink down you, but no sugar.)
  A small bowl of cereal, preferably one with bran.
  Half a grapefruit.

Lunch:
  A steak or an omelette. Mixed salad or some boiled vegetables.
  Fresh fruit.
  A glass of milk.

Tea:
  No such luck!

Supper (or Dinner if you're posh):
  Soup.
  Pasta or fish. Another salad. (Whoopee!) If it's fish then I prefer trout that I've caught myself.
  Milk or mineral water.

I don't expect you to have the same meal week-in, week-out. When we went to Italy we took a trained dietician with us from Lilleshall and I set out the sort of things he suggested below. Cheese, yoghurt, liver, eggs, chicken, they're all fine in moderation. Try not to eat too much red meat, have lots to drink (not fizzy unless it's water – even the diet pops are more fattening than water and probably give you less energy). If you have to eat bread keep to wholemeal; if you have to eat pizzas (and I do) make them small and keep off the toppings. Make sweets, chocolate, ice cream, desserts a special treat, maybe on a Sunday if you've no game. You'll soon find you can live without them, and when you have to buy a new pair of shorts because your old ones are too big for you, you'll feel so good physically you won't even worry about what it's costing you!

Foods for Soccer players

The foods listed below are examples of the ideal foods to eat at the various meal times. A selection of those listed should be chosen (not all of them!).

Breakfast
Fruit juice
Cereals:
    Cornflakes
    Weetabix
    Shredded Wheat, etc
    (NB semi-skimmed milk on cereal)
Toast (brown bread)
Low fat spread
Jam/marmalade

Avoid: eggs, bacon, fried bread, sausages, fried eggs

Main Meal
Lean meat – not fried. Ideally 'white', e.g. chicken
Potatoes – boiled, not fried
Vegetables
Rice
Pasta
    Lasagna

Spaghetti Bolognese, etc
Fish (grilled, boiled – not fried)

Avoid: chips, fried foods, salad cream, dressings, mayonnaise

Yoghurt
Fresh fruit
Rice pudding

Light Meal
Toast
Bread (sandwiches)
Pasta
Salad
Chicken
Fish

Fresh fruit (especially bananas)
Tinned fruit in syrup
Yoghurt
Fruit cake

Some points to note

1. Carbohydrates are the key ingredient in a footballer's diet. These provide the energy for training and playing. Foods high in carbohydrates include:

Potatoes
Pasta
Spaghetti
Rice
Bread
Jam/marmalade
Cereals
Bananas
Tinned fruit

2. Carbohydrates should be eaten all of the time. However it is advisable to eat extra carbohydrates during the 2–3 days before a match, and for the day after the match.

3. Avoid foods high in fat. Fat does not provide a useful energy source for football, and can easily cause a player to put on weight. Foods high in fat include:

Chips
Chocolate
Crisps
Salad cream
Mayonnaise
Butter
Biscuits
Sausages

4. Avoid fried foods. Frying introduces fat into the food, and can easily cause weight to increase.

5. Eat plenty of fresh fruit and vegetables. These help to provide the body with the vitamins and minerals which it needs to keep healthy.

EXERCISES AND WARM UP · 3

When Jack Charlton gave me dire warnings about my weight and fitness as a kid at Newcastle I panicked. I dressed myself in plastic bin liners and ran through the night until the weight poured off me, until running for ninety minutes was a holiday compared to what I put myself through. The principle was right, the practice was wrong. However, I've learned that road work is an important part of training but like everything else it has to be done in moderation. I reckon that running ten kilometres a week is enough, although some trainers have their players running cross-country every day. None of the teams I have been with as a professional really concentrates on road running nowadays, but obviously in training they will do a few laps around the pitch at some time during a session. Running itself is a way of warming up but obviously you can't go on a five kilometre run just before a match. What you do have to do is make sure that every part of your body is warmed up, toned up, ready to do its job in the match. Even if it's not a match day and you're just training you shouldn't even think of starting unless and until you've done some simple exercises.

So start off with a mild jog, shaking the body as you go along, almost skipping along. Then run sideways, a bit like a crab, turning as you go, then checking and going the opposite way. This gets your body used to sudden movements in action on the field. Change the pace to little sharp bursts of running, kicking up your heels to touch the fingers of your hand which you hold behind you.

Whatever you do, don't start stretching until you're fully warmed up. Mirandinha, my Brazilian team mate at Newcastle told me that in Brazil they'd start their training with a 10 minute jog, starting at a slow pace and gradually speeding up, just enough to get the blood nicely circulating. Nothing would be done in any quick or jerking movements until they were warm and then it was on to the sort of stretching exercises I've set out in this chapter. This kind of warm up has always been popular in South America and in Scandinavia, whereas we've been prepared to go to the pitch 10 minutes before a game, start the match and that's it.

Keep your knees up with a bit of high kicking, patting your knees as you run. Run with your arms up and down in the air, your own version of 'Let's have a disco'.

Have somebody leading you, calling 'up' or 'down'. When its up, then jump in the air heading an imaginary ball, when it's down, then go down on your haunches.

All this should have your body nicely warmed up, with the pace gradually increasing.

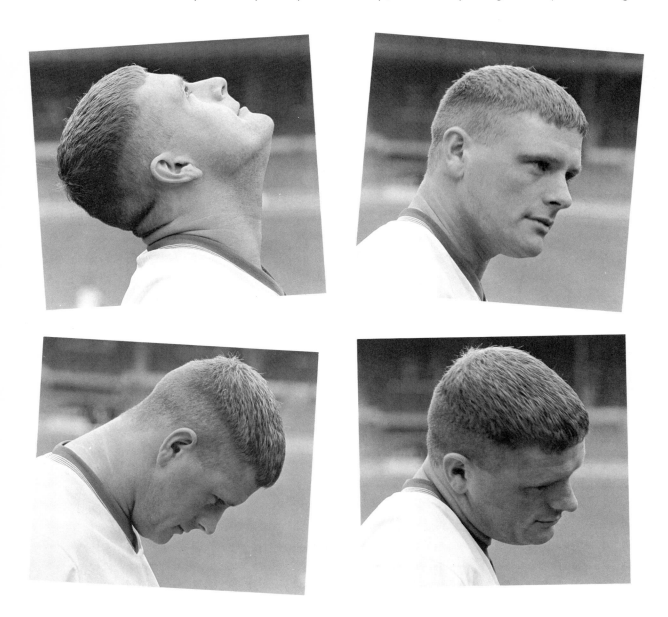

Neck exercises

As you'll see from the photographs below you must make sure that your neck muscles are as relaxed as your leg muscles. People say that I've a nervous habit on the field of moving my neck from shoulder to shoulder like a chicken. It's not nerves, it's just me making sure that no stiffness gets into my neck muscles and that when I

have to head the ball I'm not going to do myself an injury. It's amazing how much use you put your neck to in ninety minutes of football. Clearly it's the real power behind headers, and we'll show you that when we deal with heading techniques, but all the time on the pitch you're looking around, turning your head when you turn your body, thrusting your neck out when you run. Watch a running player, look at the vein standing out in his neck, look at the position of his head.

Arm exercises

Then there are your arms. Now Maradona, some people say, exercises his hands, but me, Gazza, I use my arms a lot. They're the pistons to my running machine. I know that sometimes I don't look very elegant when I'm running, but I reckon that if you use your arms properly and fairly then you can be very difficult to shake off the ball. The arm can also be used to shield off players although I know many footballers who think that the use of the arms in that way can be a foul. I love the way Stuart Hall described a goal I scored against Luton: 'Gascoigne, arms flailing like an albatross, moves into a cluster of

It's all right for the coach, he can just watch!

players. He reappears with the ball, more arms flailing, a side foot, a goal ...'
Wonderful stuff! However it's just as easy to pull a muscle in your arm as in any
other part of your anatomy, just as painful and just as effective at putting you out of
a game. Arm injuries can be the most frustrating of all; you feel fine, you feel fit but
with your arm in a sling or a cast they won't let you play. So follow the simple
exercises here before you start, and throughout the game. As you can see I'm a great

believer in touching your toes (I had to do that a lot when I was at school) and stretching your arms backward and forward across your chest, looking like a cross between a military exercise and a Jane Fonda workout. Swing your arms during the game whenever you can (obviously not in another player's face), don't just save the arm swinging for when you score! Constant movement of your neck and arms may make you look a bit funny but it's a good way of relaxing tension and a good way of keeping yourself involved and busy even when you don't have the ball.

Get yourself swaying with your left hand on your hip and your right hand in the air above your body.

Trunk exercises

Much of the strength in my game is in the sway of my hips, the movement of my trunk on and off the ball. Someone once said that if I wasn't a footballer I could make a living as a limbo dancer or a hula-hoop expert (remember them, all of you readers over 40?!). Again, I'll show you how to use the trunk of your body and your hips a bit later but right now we have to concentrate on getting your hips ready to use. My pre-match warm up for my body is shown here. Again you'll see that it involves a fair bit of touching of toes, coming back up and also, this time, rocking sideways while keeping your legs firmly positioned. I can't guarantee you'll never pull a muscle or suffer a strain but if you follow the simple steps I suggest at least you'll minimise the risk.

Leg exercises

Finally, your legs (for those of you not too good at anatomy that includes the thighs). Stand up, pull your leg back up behind you and stand on one leg. Put your arm out to give yourself balance. Stretch the leg a few times, then change legs but still do your stork impression.

Lubricants are one way of avoiding muscle strains, spasms and cramp, but personally I don't like running around the pitch with so much grease on me that I don't know whether to go out through the tunnel or make my way to the club kitchen and into an oven! It's the smell as well. Embrocations have improved, even since I've been in the game, but some of them can keep the opposition away more effectively than a couple of tough tackles. So use lubricants by all means, but not to excess, and don't use them instead of warm up exercises. They're a supplement, not a replacement.

I've set out a few more simple leg exercises which have stood me in good stead; they concentrate on helping me avoid injuries to the groin, thighs, hamstrings, ankles and calves. Although I've had a few injuries in my career none of them have been caused by failing to warm up properly. There's nothing you can do about a kick on the ankle, or a broken bone in your wrist. You *can* protect yourself though against self-induced injuries. There are enough chances out there of being hurt, so why increase them by hurting yourself?

Try crossing your feet and then bending forward to touch your toes, then reverse the crossing of the feet and bend forward again (for hamstrings). Stretch those legs to relax the hamstring – nothing's worse than having to come off during a match because of a pulled hamstring.

Relax the hamstring, even if it does look silly!

Kick each leg out side to side as if you're dancing. Don't be self-conscious, if you're loosening your muscles it doesn't matter how stupid you look – it's what's happening to your body that matters. Run fast on the spot, then try stretching the front groin. Put weight on your front leg, with it bent in front of you, keep the back leg straight out, but bounce up and down on it.

You're not finished yet. Run a couple of yards, then bend down, touch the ground, even sweep the floor with your hands. Ring the changes with a forward roll and finish up with a few more bends to touch your toes and stretching across the chest. If

Stretch the groin muscles

I don't see what's so funny! Colin Suggett's got a strange sense of humour!

Get right back to touch the back of your thighs

Above: I always wanted to be a traffic policeman!
Right: Let's have a disco!

you follow these exercises you'll be warm and sweating (yugh!) even on a cold day. If you still feel cold after all that then you've either not done them properly, or else you're dead.

So there you have it. As I've said, each person will develop their own warm up requirements. As your career progresses you'll realise just how much work you have to do before a match to make sure you fulfil your potential on the pitch.

*T*he best boots and trainers are not necessarily the most comfortable. Just because it's expensive doesn't always mean it's right for you. For years and years I got by with boots that by today's standards were really cheap – my mum worked hard even for those; they were what we could afford. That's what I got and it didn't exactly do my career any harm, did it?

The important thing is to take your time in picking a pair of boots and when you've got them to appreciate them, so don't rush into a shop when you've only five minutes to spare. Make a shopping expedition of it, save up so that it's a real treat. Try on every boot in the shop if you have to (I don't think the National Union of Shop Assistants are going to vote me the Man of the Year) but get it right. If one shop doesn't have a boot that feels right then move on to the next shop. Don't be scared or embarrassed to say no. Once you've worn them you can't take them back.

Below you'll see a picture of the sort of boot I like to wear. Puma are bringing out a whole range of them in the summer and I've worked with them all along the line so that the 'Gazza boot' is exactly the thing I would have liked to wear when I was your age. Again, though, individual tastes will vary. What's right for one person will be totally wrong for another. If that wasn't the case there wouldn't be all the different boot manufacturers about.

Once you've got your boots and trainers be proud of them

whatever they cost. Always clean your boots, even after a training session. Make sure your studs are all there and nice and even. If you've the sort of boot in which you can change the stud then carefully listen to advice on whether you should use a short or long stud. If just one of your studs is missing or worn down you'll lose your balance. Football's just as much a precision sport as motor racing, the mistakes can be just a little less fatal. Having said that, and remembering the way Arthur Cox used to shout if we got it wrong on the field, I'm not too sure which might be the more dangerous sport!

Try and make your boots and trainers last. You or your parents work hard enough for your money without having to waste it buying new equipment when, with a little bit of care and attention, your old equipment would have been still in use. Don't get carried away by new designs and trendy boots. The boot is there to do a practical job. If there's life in your old boots, if you feel comfortable in them, then keep them. One of my fellow England Internationals has worn the same pair of boots for as long as I've known him. He keeps getting them mended, and I think they've more glue than leather in them by now; but for him it's not meanness, it's not superstition, it's pure comfort.

The same principles should apply to everything you wear. Take the same care over choosing your shin guards. Again I've brought out, via Stuart Surridge, my own brand of shin pads to fit every requirement, at every level of the game. That's not meant to be an advertisement, it's merely meant to show that you have to wear a shin guard to suit you – and different people have different requirements. Ankle protectors are also necessary – and if this is beginning to sound like an introduction to American football, well that's because it's become a tough game out there, and if you can avoid serious injury by wearing a little bit of equipment that doesn't interfere with your game, then that's exactly what you should do.

Buy your shorts and shirt a little bit on the big side. There's nothing wrong in having something with a bit of growth in it, as my mum always says, and you'll also be comfortable as you run. You might think that something skin-tight shows off your fine figure (particularly if you're a female footballer) but believe me, it also slows you down.

Always keep your socks up. You might think that it looks fancy to have them rolled down around your ankles but when they're pulled up over your shin guards, not only do they keep your muscles warm, they also give you a bit of added protection.

Keep your shirt tucked in. If you're wearing a long sleeved shirt keep the sleeves rolled down. Always look tidy when you play. It creates a good impression. You get the odd fancy Dan, with his shirt sleeves flapping, his shirt over his shorts, his socks rolled down, almost inevitably with an eccentric haircut. He *needs* to attract attention with his looks rather than his play. *You* attract attention by showing off your skills in a neat tidy way. If you look neat and tidy, if you feel neat and tidy, then you'll play neat and tidy.

Headbands are also unnecessary as far as I'm concerned. Steve Foster, who made them fashionable, wore them for a purpose. He had an old head injury and it was a fashionable way of giving himself protection. Obviously if you're carrying a knock or a cut around the head, and you've been cleared fit to play, then a headband is sensible. Sweatbands can also be useful and sensible if you're prone to getting hot and sweaty in a match. You can't very well pull out a paper hanky in the middle of a match – and you should only use your shirt for special occasions – like losing in the semi-final of a World Cup!

Now that you've got all the gear, take it off – or at least take off the bits around your feet. That's right, the lot of it; boots, trainers, socks. Now do the simple exercise below in your bare feet. That's how to really get the feel of the ball. Touch and feel. It's no coincidence that so many of the successful African nations practise in bare feet. They used to play in them too, until rules and regulations insisted otherwise. It's good to practise for a quarter of an hour every day in bare feet or at least in stockinged feet. It toughens up the skin, makes the ball feel more like a part of you, it's back to nature. Don't try and tackle each other without shoes on, concentrate on the ball as shown here.

Touch and feel – with or without boots, that's the very heart of the game. Obviously, strength and power are important, but football's basically a touch sport, and if you don't feel it in your very heart then you're never going to be able to play it to the best of your potential.

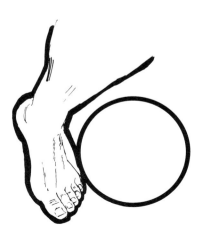

5 · CONTROL

As with everything else in life if you're out of control you take risks. Hit a bend in a car at eighty miles an hour, you may survive or you may end up a messy heap; ski down a mountain faster than you've been taught and forget how to snow plough and you could get to the bottom of a ski lift a lot faster than you intended by going over the side of the mountain. Football's no different. It's a percentage sport. Of course, you might score an outrageous goal from twenty yards with your shin – that'll be down to luck, not skill and control. It's the same as hitting a tennis smash off the wood of the racket. It may work but it won't feel good. That's how you feel when you're in control – good.

In the drawing below you'll see I've set up some cones. Now I don't expect you to have training cones in your back garden, I don't expect you to go out on to the motorway and 'borrow' them either. Any obstacle will do – deck chairs, spades, garden gnomes (although be sure not to hurt them – I've two gnomes in my own front garden and I get someone in to feed and clean them while I'm away). Training with cones (or gnomes for that matter) needn't be boring – indeed there are some cones (and gnomes) who make more sense than some of the people I've met in football! So play the cone game and develop your ball control.

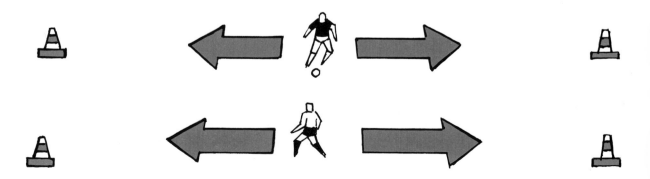

Each player works between two cones set opposite each other. You move the ball and you'll see you also move your opponent, trying to get him off balance and then exploit the situation. You can even imagine he's the goalkeeper and you're pulling him out of position. Your object is to end up with the ball under control touching one of your cones, before he can get near the cone opposite.

I've also set out a square drill. For this you need some other people; again it won't only improve your control and sharpen your reactions but it'll also be enjoyable. As I said, do this with four people. Three players go on the outside along the lines of a square. One is in the middle. Each player is allowed two touches of the ball. The one in the middle has to cut off, pass it and intercept. This exercise develops free movement on and off the ball. Whoever's pass is intercepted has to move into the middle. This exercise can also be done in a circle.

Try making a circle with half a dozen of you using three balls. Only move within the circle. Call out to whom you're passing. They take over and repeat the action. Try and concentrate on the ball, while at the same time try not to get in each other's way. Develop that into a game of 'musical balls' so that the six of you have to battle for the balls in the circle. When the 'music stops' – or the whistle blows – if you haven't got a ball then you drop out, and the number of balls is reduced. Finally there'll just be two of you with one ball – who'll survive? This exercise develops lots of different skills, such as control, movement off the ball, reverse turns, takeovers and individual tricks.

Before you set off on any kind of run or indeed before you attempt to pass you must first of all control the ball. The first touch is the most important touch of all. Often you've only a split second to do it and trapping and passing almost become one movement. If you follow the diagrams you'll see I've tried to take you step by step through the basics of trapping the ball, both when standing still and when running. What you're going to do with it once you've trapped it will sometimes determine how to trap it. You've heard people say there's more than one way to skin a cat – well there's certainly more than one way to trap a ball.

As you can see, you can use various parts of your body to trap and control the ball, but whichever part you use the basic need is to take the pace off it. That you can do, by almost taking away the relevant bit of you just before the ball hits you. A good way to practise trapping, if you don't have a friend to play with, is to use a wall or a door. Although this isn't going to make me any friends amongst parents, you can even do it in your bedroom with a foam ball, just getting yourself familiar with where you make the ball hit you, to allow you to do with the ball exactly what you want. As I said before, it's touch and feel every time.

When using the sole you have to try and anticipate where the ball will bounce. To help you, put your non-kicking foot on the ground, a bit to the left of where you think the ball will land. Raise your kicking foot so that the thigh is

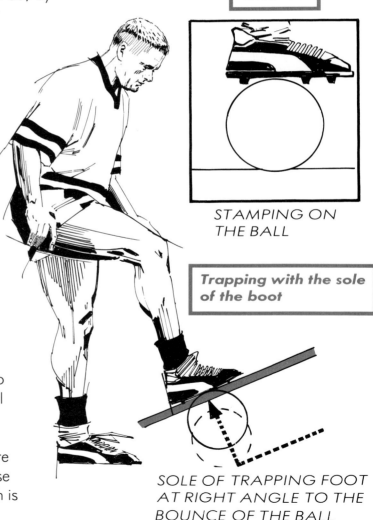

WRONG

STAMPING ON THE BALL

Trapping with the sole of the boot

SOLE OF TRAPPING FOOT AT RIGHT ANGLE TO THE BOUNCE OF THE BALL

at almost ninety degrees to your body, then as the ball reaches the ground put the sole of your kicking foot over the top of the ball about five centimetres above it. Try and keep the sole at right angles to the direction at which the ball will leave the ground.

Above: Collecting the ball on the instep

When you use the instep to trap the ball, again you have to guess where the ball will land. This time have your body facing the ball leaning forward slightly. The non-kicking foot goes alongside the landing point of the ball. The inside of the kicking foot sweeps towards the landed ball.

Right: Cushion ball with thigh on impact

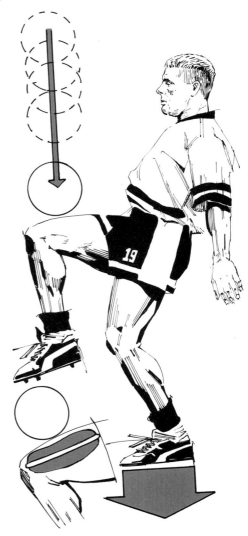

Left: Cushion ball with chest on impact

Right: Trapping at speed, while running

Right: Trapping with the outside of the foot and moving off in the same action

Left: Trapping with the inside of the foot

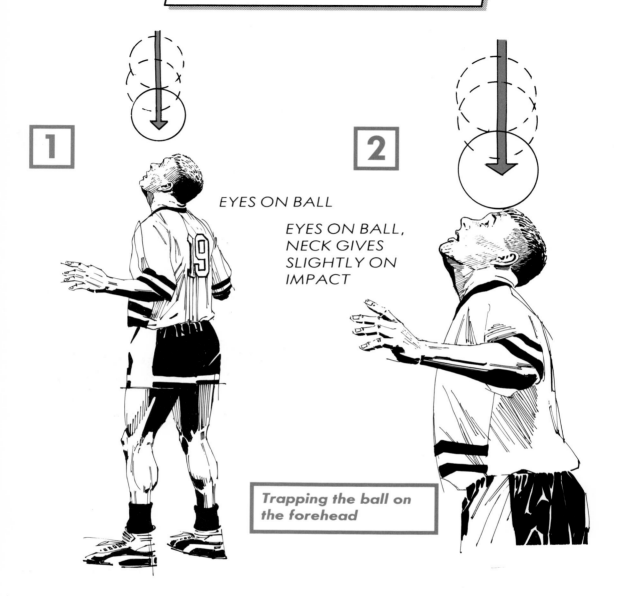

EYES ON BALL

EYES ON BALL,
NECK GIVES
SLIGHTLY ON
IMPACT

**Trapping the ball on
the forehead**

Use the various techniques to have cone races (opposite). Divide yourselves into two teams. The ball's thrown in to the first member. He controls it and sets off on his run, weaving between the cones. He finishes with a pass to the next in line who also sets off. First team to finish wins, the losing team has to do a lap of the pitch. That's the way it goes!

1

2

Forward moving chest trap

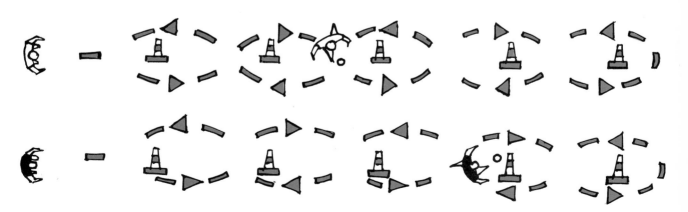

Cone races

I can beat the cone, but I'm not too sure about the kid

38

KICKING • 6

If you look up the verb 'kick' in a dictionary you'll see it says: 'To strike out with the foot … to drive or move things by striking with the foot,' or, specifically with regard to football, 'to score by a kick'. Yet there's so much more to kicking than simply applying a foot covered by leather against another piece of simulated leather – that sounds quite posh doesn't it? Maybe I'll be offered a column in *The Times* when this book is published!

The first thing to say is that I rarely, nowadays, kick the ball with the toe of the boot. When I was a kid that was the first bit of your boot that got worn out. (Or your shoe if you didn't have a boot – and played in the street with your school shoes, and then got a right rucking from your mum because she'd only just bought you those shoes and knew you were going to go out in the rain with half the sole hanging off!!). I might use the toe for a lob or a chip on the goalie as shown here but apart from that it's always the inside or the outside of the foot, or the heel if I feel particularly cheeky. With the chip you do have to get your toe right underneath the ball, giving it a bit of back spin just with the shape of your foot. Get your body sideways around the ball.

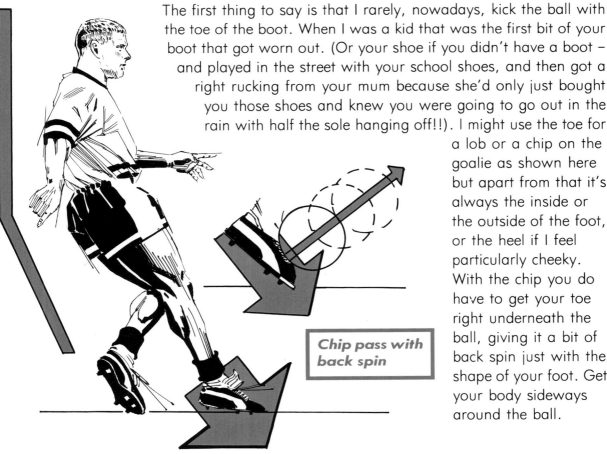

Chip pass with back spin

39

Everybody says cricket's a sideways on game, but so's football in many ways.

As with almost everything else in the game kicking is a question of touch and feel. It's almost the first thing you learn to do as a baby – to kick. Most professional players will have their dim and distant memory of somebody seeing them kick a toy brick or a soft ball and saying 'He's a natural'. Not everybody can be a professional but if you're going to go anywhere in the sport you'll have to have a naturally good kicking technique.

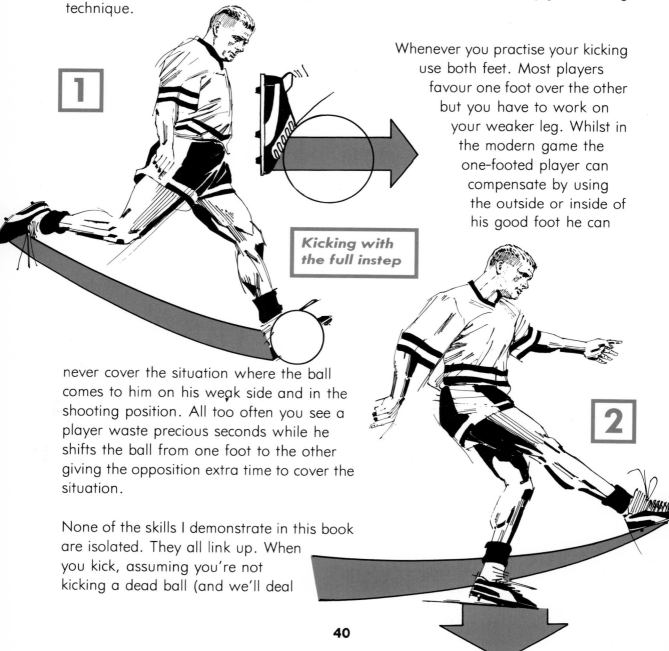

1

Kicking with the full instep

Whenever you practise your kicking use both feet. Most players favour one foot over the other but you have to work on your weaker leg. Whilst in the modern game the one-footed player can compensate by using the outside or inside of his good foot he can

2

never cover the situation where the ball comes to him on his weak side and in the shooting position. All too often you see a player waste precious seconds while he shifts the ball from one foot to the other giving the opposition extra time to cover the situation.

None of the skills I demonstrate in this book are isolated. They all link up. When you kick, assuming you're not kicking a dead ball (and we'll deal

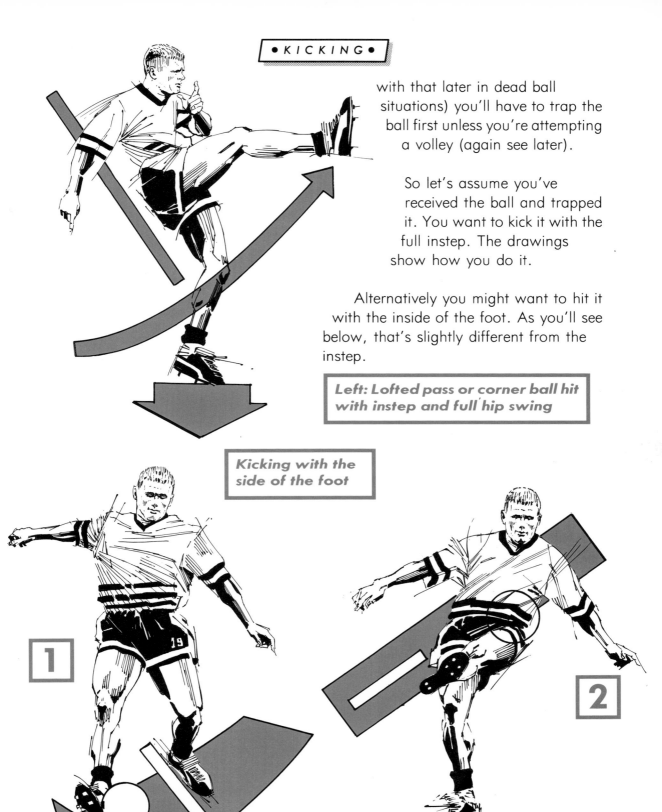

with that later in dead ball situations) you'll have to trap the ball first unless you're attempting a volley (again see later).

So let's assume you've received the ball and trapped it. You want to kick it with the full instep. The drawings show how you do it.

Alternatively you might want to hit it with the inside of the foot. As you'll see below, that's slightly different from the instep.

Left: Lofted pass or corner ball hit with instep and full hip swing

Kicking with the side of the foot

1

2

Kicking with the outside of the instep or heeling the ball off have totally different results and can be effective passes, the power coming from the ankle.

The outside of the foot also has a purpose. As you'll see, the left and the right foot produce different results. When I hit the ball to Steve Bull for him to score against Czechoslovakia that was a pass with the outside of my right foot.

At first you'll have to concentrate on exactly which part of the foot you use to kick the ball – and which foot you use. If you're one-footed you have to try and make yourself use your 'dead' foot. This takes concentration and will-power. If you're good at history at school but lousy at physics it's much more tempting to do your history homework than your physics. All that does is make you better at history and worse at physics. It's the same with the use of your feet. One thing I've learned in football is never take the easy option. Try out a game where you're not allowed to use your good foot. Assuming you're right-footed, even if the ball goes on your right side, unless you can move across to hit it with your left foot, you have to let the ball go past you. Try playing in one boot and one slipper, the boot on your weak foot and the slipper on your good foot. Another exercise I used to try when I was a kid was to go to a park on my own, find an empty pitch with the goal posts up and try and hit the cross bar with shots from my weak foot. I think you're probably beginning to realise you can't get anywhere in football unless you work at it.

BALANCING NON-KICKING LEG

Surprise back heel crossing one leg over the other

Now you want to try your trapping and kicking techniques with some friends. Split into two lines on either side of the goal to vary the angle of the ball coming in. Have somebody on each side throwing the ball in for you to trap and then kick. At this stage don't worry about power, concentrate on accuracy.

HEADING • 7

Babies might
kick bricks and balls
but they don't
usually head them,
which goes to show that
kicking is natural but heading is
not – and therefore it needs
more work on it. Most kids are
scared to head the ball at first and
why not? When you watch the
game on TV some six-foot lunatic is
belting a hard round object at you as
hard as he can and you're being
asked to put your head in the way.
Although I never played in the days
when balls were made of tough
leather and had laces I can just
imagine the pain of a muddy lace
in the eyes. That doesn't happen any
more, and heading the ball hurts no
more than kicking it, provided you hit
the ball in the right place and keep
your eye on it – yes, right up to the very
moment of impact. You just have to resist
the temptation to close your eyes and hope
for the best because the result will not be what
you want. If you're lucky the ball will just go
straight up in the air – if you're unlucky it'll take
your head off!

**Keep your eye on
the ball**

43

For the most part it's the forehead you use to head the ball, no other part of the head, and you have to feel confident about it. If you like, start out with a sponge ball, or a small 'fun' training ball. (Yes you've guessed, Stuart Surridge does make a small Gazza Skill Ball.) Once you're satisfied that you're hitting the ball on the correct spot you can move on to the real thing.

The only time you'll use the top of your head is for flick ons. This is a question of timing. It's almost like tossing your head back to clear some hair out of your eye.

The flick-on header can be very effective in the penalty box from a corner. Some teams, Wimbledon in particular, have scored many goals by using that technique.

You have to relax when you're heading. If you're tense with your eyes closed then the head dips and your shoulders are hunched. The drawing shows what happens then.

Heading is also a question of balance. In order to head properly you have to be able to jump properly and then land well balanced, ready for the next move in the game. The ball may come straight back to you from your header out and you're absolutely no use to anybody if you're sprawled on the ground, admiring the handiwork of your own header.

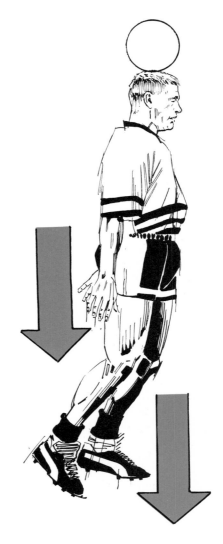

Sometimes it's difficult to play balls along the ground, particularly when the opposition packs its defence. That's when heading ability in front can become absolutely vital. Heading can be used as a method of attack or defence or control. Jack Charlton's motto of 'Keep the ball in the air – play to God' may at times not produce pretty football but it can be very effective. If you're looking at individuals, Gary Mabbutt, Terry Butcher, Steve Foster and Mark Wright are all masters of the defensive header, while some of the performances of Mark Hateley, Steve Bull, Niall Quinn and Paul Stewart demonstrate the unsettling effect on defences of aggressive heading ability up front. The good defensive header should also be able to turn defence into attack, often more speedily than the use of the foot. Get your arms up to give yourself height and velocity, use the whole of the top half of your body. It's almost a swimming motion as you stretch for that ball, flicking your neck at just the right moment. It's balance, power and timing.

I've shown here several tactical examples of the use of the header in both defensive and attacking situations.

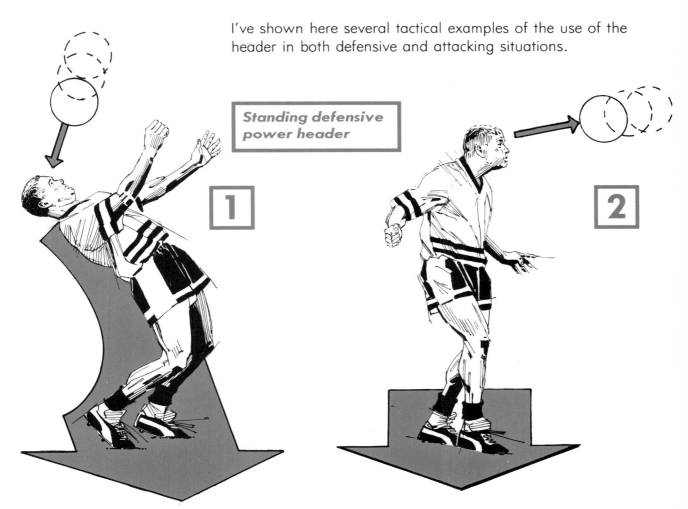

Standing defensive power header

1

2

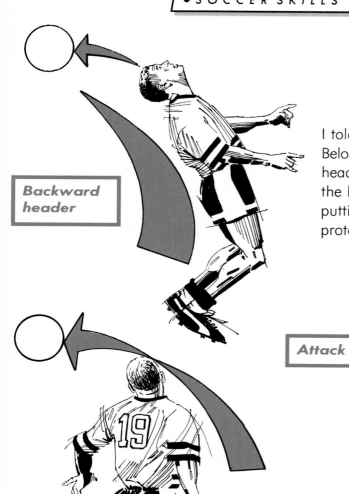

Backward header

I told you before about neck exercises. Below you see how useful they'll be as your head must nod forward quite forcibly to hit the ball. Get real muscle into it, while putting your arm out for balance and protection from elbows.

Attack the ball

Flick-on header

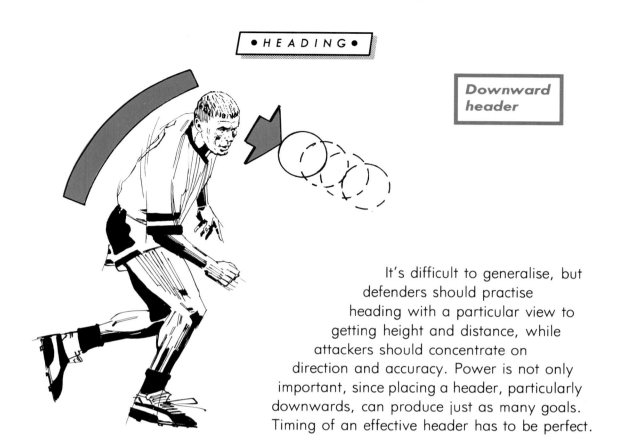

Downward header

It's difficult to generalise, but defenders should practise heading with a particular view to getting height and distance, while attackers should concentrate on direction and accuracy. Power is not only important, since placing a header, particularly downwards, can produce just as many goals. Timing of an effective header has to be perfect.

You see much more heading in the English game than on the Continent. Although that doesn't particularly suit my natural style of play, it is an aspect of my game that I've worked on indirectly; in other words I've practised knocking the ball into the penalty area so that other players can score with headers. Let them do all the jumping! The famous free kick against Belgium in Bologna could just as easily have been headed in by someone else as volleyed in so brilliantly by David Platt. Then, of course, there was the free kick against Egypt which Mark Wright headed into the goal.

It's not generally known that when I was in the Newcastle Youth team that won the Youth Cup I was actually the target man for headers, rather than Joe Allon (although that didn't stop Joe scoring loads of goals, which he continued to do at Hartlepool).

To practise your heading, quite a useful exercise is to have someone behind the goal throw balls to three or four of you, who not only take turns in heading, but also try alternately jumping with both legs, then with the right only, and finally with the left. You can ring the changes by having the thrower stand on either side of the goal with the ball then coming in diagonally. It can also be varied to tie in with free kicks and corner practice for two other players who pump balls in; or else the coach (having given each player a number) shouts the number and the individual has to go for the header. That sort of work also helps to improve your positional sense, as well as giving you practice in near-post headers and diving headers.

Another good game to play is throw, catch and head. Divide yourselves into two teams on a mini-pitch with real goals. Each side has to throw the ball to start the game, then head it, then catch it, in that order. You can only score with the head. If you break the sequence the ball goes to the other team, or else they can try and intercept. It gets really funny when the ball hits the ground and you have to get down on your knees to head it along!

The diving header is sometimes thought of as flashy and dangerous. I reckon it's a real skill that shows great bravery. Nobody does it better than my team mate Gary Lineker; sometimes I'm amazed he doesn't get his head kicked off as he goes in where angels fear to tread. The diving header needs enormous courage. Basically you have to keep your eye on the ball as ever and just concentrate, concentrate, concentrate while ignoring the feet and goalkeeper's fists flying around you.

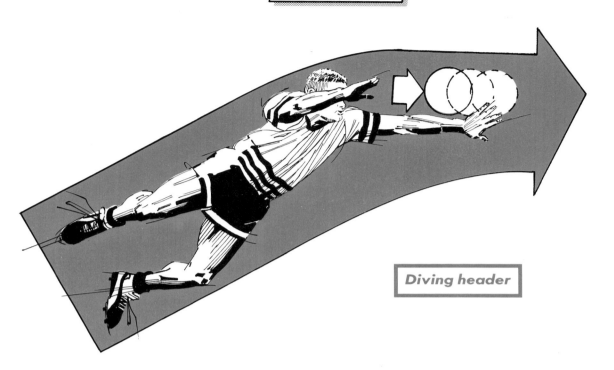

Diving header

8 • PASSING AND VISION

Football is a team game. Sometimes you have to decide to go it alone, sometimes to pass – more often than not a decision has to be made in a split second and sometimes it'll be right, sometimes wrong. On occasions I've been accused of being greedy but it's very easy to criticise when you're sitting in the stands. I don't think I'm a greedy player and I would never encourage anyone else to be. However, don't pass just for the sake of passing. There are coaches around who say get rid of the ball as soon as you get it – run off the ball, not with it. I don't think you can or should lay down general principles like that. What you do need though is to be aware of what's going on in the field around you, and to have movement off the ball. If you're standing still you're easy to mark. I'll deal with that aspect later (losing defenders) but right now we're talking about you knowing and seeing at all times where your team mates are and being able to pass to them, not only accurately, but also constructively. It's not difficult to hit a ball straight across the park in your half when all the opposition are in their half. It might bring oohs and aahs from the crowd but where does it get you? Nowhere. You're in the same attacking position but on the other side of the pitch. All you've done is shift the responsibility for going forward. Big deal!

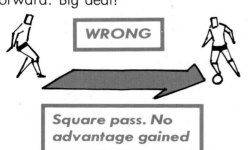

WRONG

Square pass. No advantage gained

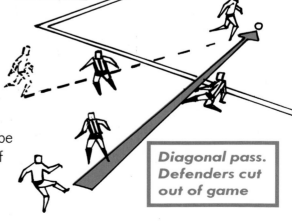

RIGHT

Diagonal pass. Defenders cut out of game

If you're going for a long pass you should be aiming either to split a defence with one of your team mates running on to it (try and apply backspin with your instep)...

Obvious passes ignored.
Instead, a diagonal pass
directed into the path of a blind
side run sets up a goal chance

... or else to cause chaos in the penalty
area.

The diagonal ball is always going
to be more of a problem than a
cross ball or a
straightforward pass.
I've shown a few of
the movements
you can do
using the
long ball.

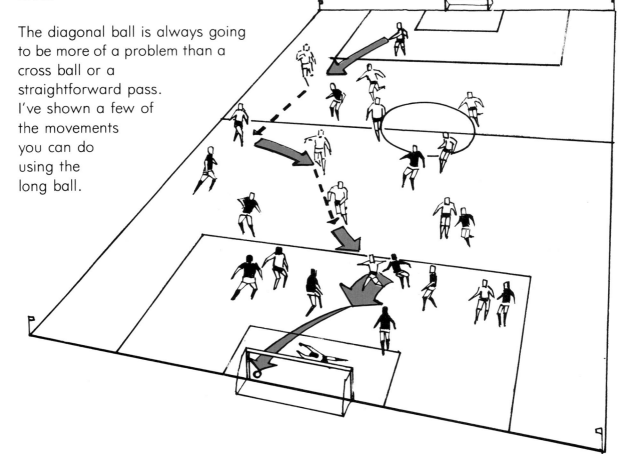

What I don't like to see is a long ball out of defence that simply goes over the head of the midfield. Football's a bit like a chain reaction, like passing buckets of water in a fire. The keeper rolls the ball to one of the back four who makes some progress down the flank from an overlap, then plays a diagonal forward ball to the midfielder. The midfielder makes ground, while his team mates move off the ball, he plays another forward pass (I'll come to 1–2s later), the striker gets the ball with his back to goal, has the ability to turn his man and scores. Now that's fast, flowing, attacking football shown on the previous page.

Practise that first of all without opposition. Then try it with the opposition knowing what you're going to do. They'll still find it hard to stop you.

The long pass may look spectacular but there are times when the short pass will be more effective. You often hear the TV commentator say, 'He signalled that pass'. What they mean is that the player has done the obvious, allowing the opposition to nip in and intercept. My game is based on not doing the obvious, but before you can achieve that you have to realise what the obvious is. (Does that make sense? It does? Good!) The illustrations on the previous pages show you what I think would be the obvious pass and then what the alternatives are. Sometimes you can fool your opponents by seeming to do the obvious. It's only when they realise that you've hit the ball with the part of the foot they weren't expecting that they also realise the ball isn't going where they expected – by then it's too late. Always have a look around you before the ball comes so when it comes you can play it off straight away. If there's nothing on for anybody else then keep hold of it, don't pass just for the sake of passing – it only takes

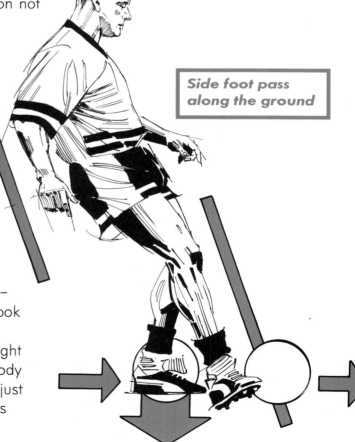

Side foot pass along the ground

1

2

Back heel pass

Surprise pass crossing one leg behind the other

BALANCE
NON-KICKING
LEG

pressure off you and puts pressure on everybody else. Practise the side foot pass, and the driven pass using the top of your foot i.e. the instep.

The passes I've shown so far depend on your passing and someone else receiving. Now let's move on to the 1–2s which involve you and one (and sometimes two) other player or players. As you'll see from the drawing, 1–2s rely on players understanding each other and need loads of practice. There's nothing worse than playing a 1–2 and not being there on the receiving end.

Everybody involved looks silly and the sort of gestures you give or get don't do a lot for team morale.

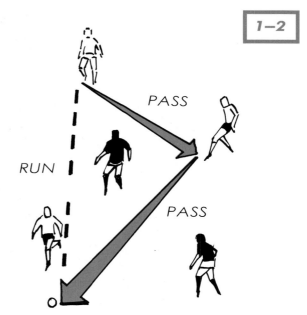

PASS

RUN

PASS

Most of the passing techniques and movements rely on team understanding, on first touches, on feeling at one with the rest of your team – there you are, it's touch and feel again. Usually when a team is allowed to play free from injuries, suspensions and transfers, they eventually get their game together. That's down to understanding, you knowing where your team mates will be at any given minute, them knowing what you're going to do, being there to assist you and receive from you. It's hard to illustrate that in a book like this but there's a message to managers and coaches. If you thought a player was good enough to get into the side in the first place be patient with him and the rest of the side. Let them bed down. Give them a run, not as individuals but as a team. If they work together on and off the field sooner or later they'll start winning. Winning, like losing, is a habit and once you start, you don't stop.

Another effective pass is the one 'down the line'. It's something I really enjoy doing because often it enables one of the wide players to get into a position where they can cross the ball into the box. It needs movement and speed on the part of the receiver as well as immediate control. As the passer you need to make sure the ball is properly weighted, sometimes by putting spin on it, sometimes by curving it, in order to place it into the run of the player going down the line. There's nothing more frustrating than chasing a ball that's been overhit. It wastes opportunity and it wastes energy. Football nowadays is played at such a pace in this country that you have to conserve every bit of energy, you've got to see yourself through ninety minutes – and that holds good no matter how hard you train. I'll show you the ideal ball down the line and how to use it once you've got it. The position of the receiver when the ball's in play is important. He has to know the ball is coming because if he's facing the wrong way and needs to turn he'll lose that vital split second that could give him the edge over the defender.

Effective passes down the line

Now that I've set out the principles you need to try some practice. Passing in pairs is a good way to start.

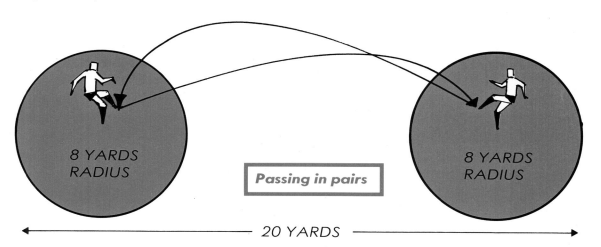

8 YARDS
RADIUS

Passing in pairs

8 YARDS
RADIUS

← 20 YARDS →

Piggy in the middle may be good fun – as long as you're not the piggy. You can play that in a circle with the players either having two touches or one and then having to pass. If you give the ball away then you go in the middle. It not only improves your passing but also your first time control.

9 • SHOOTING

'Shoot on sight', they used to say in the cowboy films I saw when I was a kid. My sister Anna reckons I never saw any films because whenever she wanted to watch a movie my brother, my dad and I always insisted on watching the sport. However, the fact I can remember at least that line shows that she's wrong.

Well, shooting on sight is not necessarily right for modern football. It's difficult enough to get a sight of goal, without wasting the opportunity when you're not in the best position. To have a shot at goal you must have a chance to score, otherwise you should hold the ball up or pass to someone who's in a better position than you. There are exceptions to this. Clive Allen, who's scored 49 goals in one season for Spurs, always shot on sight and I think the statistics show that 40 of his goals were first time shots. We're not all Clive Allen and things haven't gone so well for him since that one glorious season but the player who has a reputation of shooting on sight tends to get closed down much more quickly by the opposition.

By now you'll realise what I meant when I said that football was a chain reaction game. Each skill leads into the other and is equally important if you're going to be an all-round player. In American football they have guys who are just kickers, who sit on the touch line for most of the game and who just come on to take the kicks at goal. English football can't afford that luxury and somebody who can just kick, but who can't pass, tackle or head wouldn't last very long at any level of the game.

Let's first look at kicking a moving ball. Commentators and writers often talk about a 'brilliantly volleyed goal'. So what is a volley, and why does it need special practice? The drawing on page 58 shows the right position of the body and the feet for the perfectly executed volley either with the inside or the outside of the foot. You'll see how important it is to get your body right over the ball. If you've ever learnt skiing you know you have to get forward or else you fall over. If your body's over the ball when you shoot it keeps low, if you lean back the ball flies high. One of the best

Clive Allen shoots on sight and scores for Spurs against Watford in the 1986/87 FA Cup semi-final

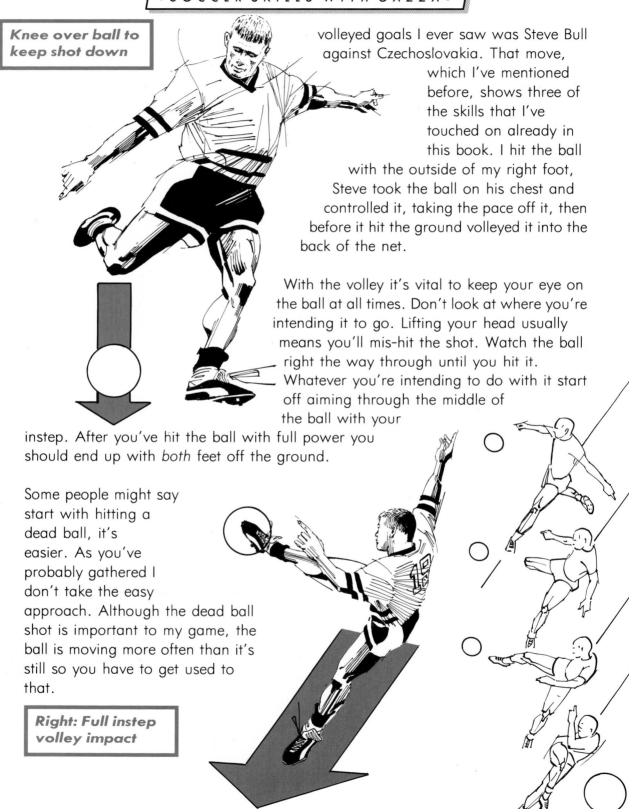

Knee over ball to keep shot down

volleyed goals I ever saw was Steve Bull against Czechoslovakia. That move, which I've mentioned before, shows three of the skills that I've touched on already in this book. I hit the ball with the outside of my right foot, Steve took the ball on his chest and controlled it, taking the pace off it, then before it hit the ground volleyed it into the back of the net.

With the volley it's vital to keep your eye on the ball at all times. Don't look at where you're intending it to go. Lifting your head usually means you'll mis-hit the shot. Watch the ball right the way through until you hit it. Whatever you're intending to do with it start off aiming through the middle of the ball with your

instep. After you've hit the ball with full power you should end up with *both* feet off the ground.

Some people might say start with hitting a dead ball, it's easier. As you've probably gathered I don't take the easy approach. Although the dead ball shot is important to my game, the ball is moving more often than it's still so you have to get used to that.

Right: Full instep volley impact

Power drive from a stationary ball. Both feet off the ground, perfect balance

Shooting is all about accuracy, so try practising either with a small goal or else by chalking numbers against a wall and making up your mind which one you're going to hit. If you hit it you score that number, if you miss then you deduct the number you actually hit. No cheating! Remember if you're on your own and you cheat, the only person you're cheating is yourself.

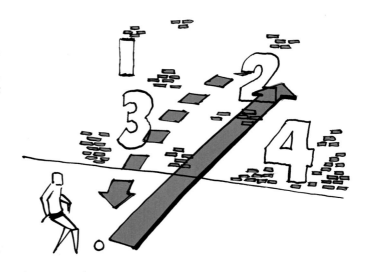

Volleys can be spectacular and even the best player is more likely to miss

the target than hit simply because of the speed with which the ball arrives and the accuracy required for the moment of impact. Once again it's all about timing.

The half volley can be more tricky than the volley because here you're hitting the ball a fraction of a second after it hits the ground but before it has time to bounce away. A good example of a goal scored with a spectacular half volley was John Barnes' effort against Uruguay. It's only experience, linked with a bit of instinct, that will tell you whether it's best to smash a volley, trap and shoot, or hit the half volley. The half volley is also about timing and accuracy. Assuming the ball comes to you fast enough it will already have its own power. Consequently try and concentrate on connecting at the right time and place, rather than taking the keeper's head off. The half volley's an exception to the rule of shooting. Don't lean over the ball, lean back, but keep your toes pointed down. Sounds a bit like a ballet lesson doesn't it? Well I've never tried it in tutus but believe me, after you've practised it for a while it's all a lot simpler than it sounds. Too many coaches and text books complicate what is really a very simple game – I don't want to add to that number.

Some of my goals from what the media describe as 'impossible angles' have got a lot of publicity, but if you're in that sort of position on the bye-line it's usually better to pull the ball back than have a shot yourself. However, I'll show you here how best to have a go from an angle, but only use that technique if you can see some daylight between the goalkeeper and the post.

No, I'm not taking off. I've just completed a volleyed shot

10. SHOTS WITH A DIFFERENCE

Goalkeepers, nowadays, are good. To somebody like me, who is trying to score goals, they seem to be getting better with every match so you have to try something different to beat them when sheer power and pace might not be enough. Sometimes you *can* do it just by hitting the ball very hard. Incredibly enough I did that with a free kick against Peter Shilton when Spurs played Derby in the 1990/91 season.

But nine times out of ten a keeper, given time, will save a hard shot. So you just have to think of something different and that's where curving, swerving and dipping the ball come into play. Those sort of shots are a bit like spin bowling in cricket, the best balls are those that are heavily disguised. Disguise equals surprise and the worst thing that you can do is think about what you're going to do for too long because that just signals it to the opposition – and the keeper in particular. Most keepers watch the eyes of the attacker. Look away from where you're going to hit the ball and that will confuse the keeper.

Assuming you're hitting the ball with your right foot, to curve the ball to the left hit the ball with the inside of your right foot. To curve the ball to the right hit the ball with the outside of your right foot.

Obviously, the opposite applies when using your left foot. Remember that it's not just kicking that decides where the ball is going to go, it's your body and your non-kicking foot as well, and most of all it's your mind. If you concentrate, if you feel comfortable with yourself and the ball, then it's far more likely to go where you intend it. Always aim a few feet to the side of where you want the ball to go, to the left if it's swinging in from the left, to the right if it's curving in from the right.

A curving shot will mean from right to left or left to right. A dipper will go up, and hopefully come down when the keeper least expects it. At the worst you should have him reaching for the crossbar trying to tip the ball over, and at least you'll get a

Gazza beats his man on his way to a hat trick against Derby in the 3—0 win for Spurs in September 1990

corner to keep up the pressure on the other team.

The ideal ball to dip is one that bounces right in front of you. You need a bit of height to the ball as you need to get your foot underneath in order to lift it. Basically, what you're applying is top spin and that's what makes the ball come down so dramatically. Some players just use their toes, but I prefer the flat at the top of the foot just behind the toe – I'm sure a few experts will write in to tell me the right name for that part of the body; I always reckoned when I did biology at school (very briefly I may say) that if you knew where it was and what to do with it then it didn't really matter very much what it was called! Anyway, back to dipping the ball; I've shown below how to do it and how to get the right effect. This is something you really have to practise with someone else, probably two people – one to throw you the ball so it bounces properly and the other in goal. If not, it's an awful long walk to keep fetching the ball and bringing it back – unless you can train a dog with a very big mouth.

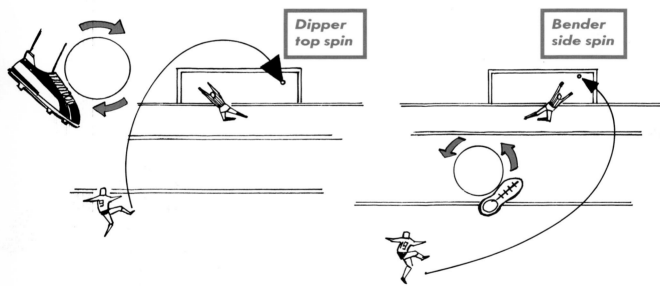

Dipper top spin

Bender side spin

Another surprise shot is the overhead kick. This can be used either as a way out of defence or as a surprise shot on goal. If you're standing with your back to goal and the ball is either bouncing in front of you or is dropping at your feet, then the defence and the keeper will think you're going to trap, turn and shoot, or pass. They'll position themselves accordingly. If in fact you shoot, you've a good chance of taking everybody by surprise if you can only get the ball on target – that can be a big if. On the other hand if it works it looks brilliant – when it doesn't you end up flat on your back feeling really stupid.

As you'll see from the drawing (over) your non-kicking foot should be almost a whole leg's length away from where your kicking foot will hit the ball. The knee should be bent. Your kicking leg should be at full stretch, with your toes reaching for the ball. In fact the point of impact with the ball should be the flat of your foot behind the toe (the bit I don't know the name of). Your toes should bend towards your instep (no, this is not some kind of joke – and no, you don't have to be double-jointed). The bent knee of the non-kicking leg will make sure your body leans backwards. You have to be confident enough to follow right through. It's a bit like a backward roll over a horse in the gym. Once you're falling backwards then bend your elbows and spread your hands (and in particular your left arm) to break your fall, rather than breaking your back or dislocating your shoulder. Two players who play the overhead kick to perfection are Hugo Sanchez, the Mexican International and Mark Hughes of Manchester United and Wales. You can either practise this on your own by throwing the ball up in front of you, or else by having a friend throwing it in. I think the use of the friend is better just to help pick you up if you do break anything!

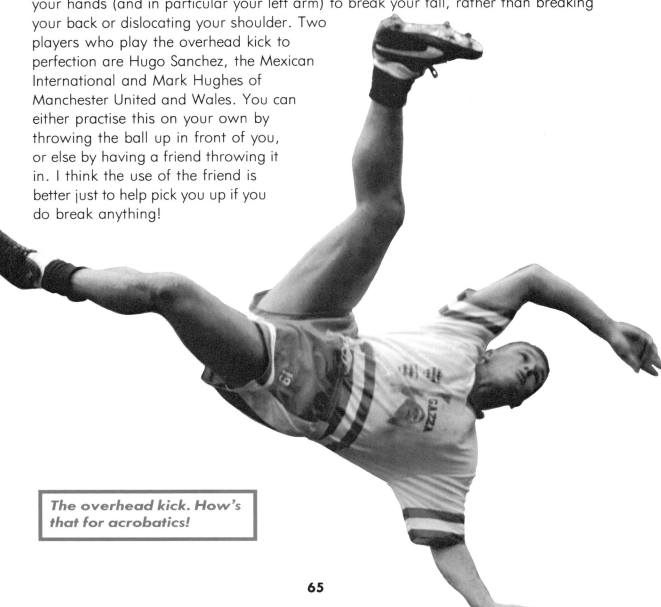

The overhead kick. How's that for acrobatics!

Overhead volley

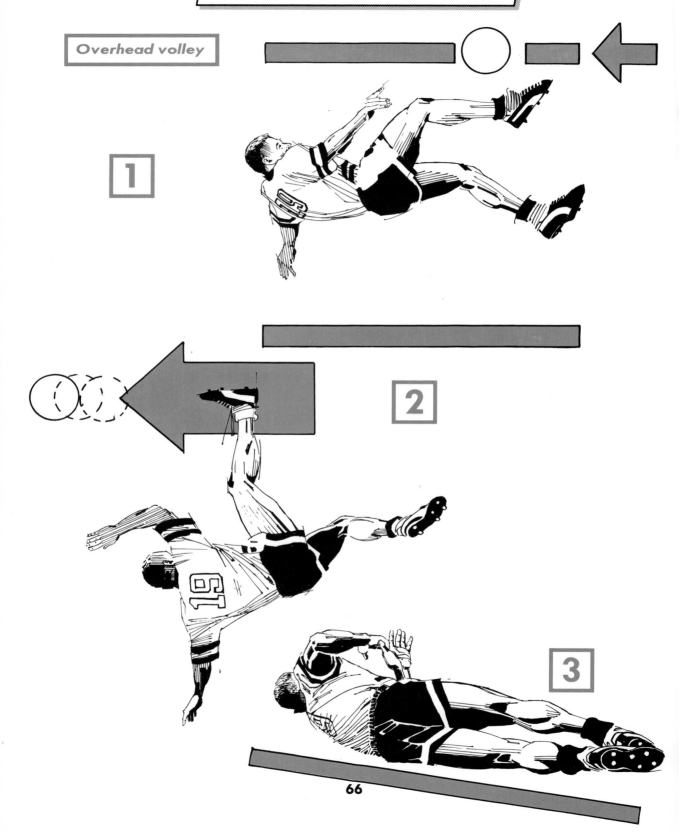

1

2

3

Overhead clearance

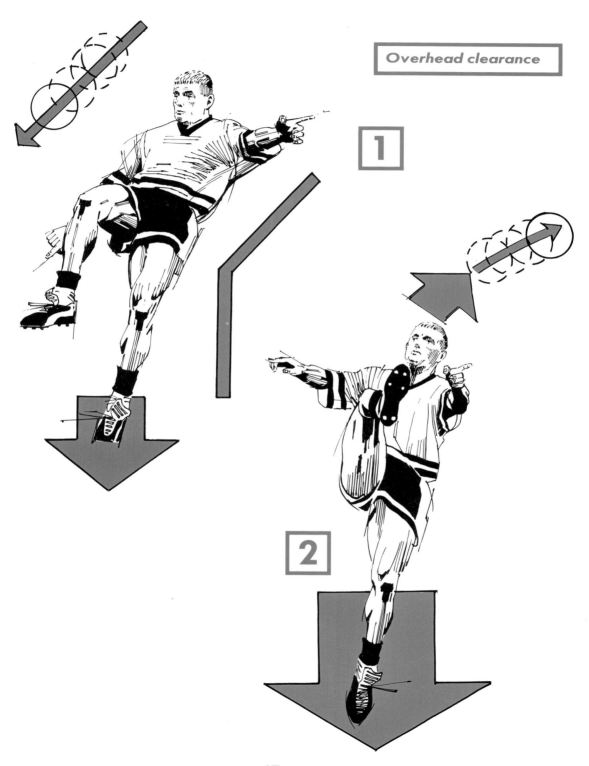

1

2

11 • DEAD BALLS

Logically it should be easier to kick a dead ball than one that's moving; but logic doesn't have anything to do with football. Of course it's easier to make contact, but it's what you do with it that's important. Kicking a still ball is not just a matter of seeing how far and how high you can propel it; you have to make good use of it, and how good a use you can put a free kick to depends to a certain extent on whether or not your team mates know what you're going to do with the ball. You must remember that the ability to kick a dead ball is very important because a large percentage of goals are scored from what we in the game call 'restarts' and what most commentators call dead ball situations.

Obviously the two free kicks that have given me the most pleasure in my career were those that produced the goals against Belgium and Egypt.

Anywhere between the halfway line and the penalty area is where I specialise in my free kicks. Depending on the distance, think carefully as to whether or not you'ze going to take a shot or pump the ball into the penalty area. If you think it's right to shoot, then do it. Never be afraid to miss. Although I never played alongside

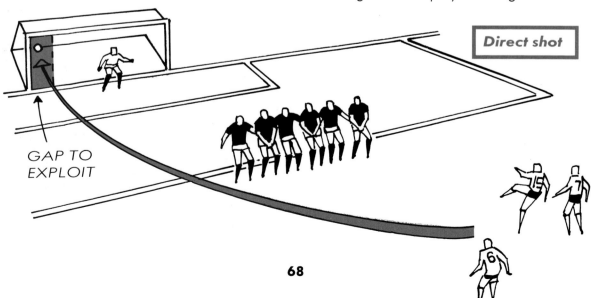

GAP TO
EXPLOIT

Direct shot

68

David Platt scores the 119th minute winner against Belgium in Bologna. Victories don't come closer than that

Malcolm Macdonald at Newcastle, and although I certainly don't agree with a lot of the things he's said about me and those around me, one thing he did say has always stuck in my mind: 'If you don't shoot at goal, you can't score.' Whether you're playing midfield or up front, one of the important modern statistics is 'attempts on goal'. Whether or not it's right to shoot from a direct free kick depends on the position of the defensive wall and the goalkeeper, and whether you have the ability either to swerve the ball around the wall, or else to place it over the wall and into the net beyond the keeper.

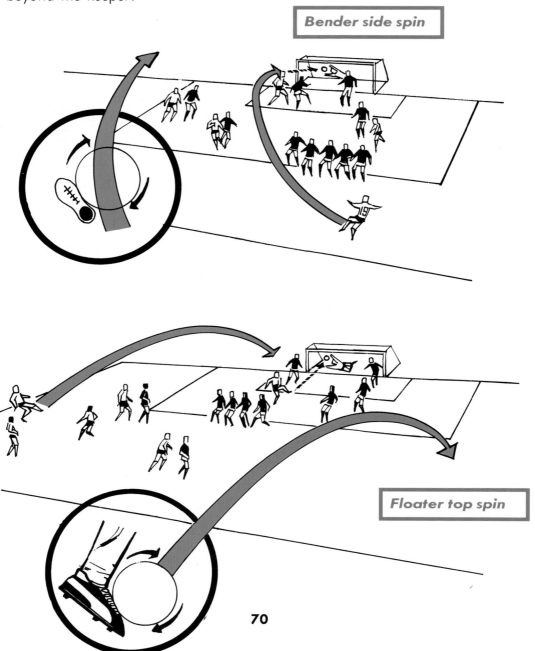

Bender side spin

Floater top spin

70

Mark Wright heads the vital winner for England against Egypt from Gazza's free kick

When I'm taking a free kick from a distance I prefer to put pace and swerve on the ball, really to fire the ball in. It might make it just that bit harder for my team mates to control but it increases the chances of evading the opposition. I think my favourite free kick situation is halfway into the opposition half, on either wing. You just have so many options from that position.

The floater is one of those options. Here, rather than using pace, you get the ball to hold up in the air a little bit. You have to adapt your game slightly to weather conditions and there's no doubt that, on a windy day, a ball floating into the box can cause chaos – as even you don't quite know where it's going to land. I've set out opposite just how to float the ball in and as you'll see, once again, there's that element of top spin.

12 · *CORNERS AND PENALTIES*

When you see me, or any other player lifting an arm or two before we take a corner that's a signal to our team mates telling them what sort of corner it's going to be. Now I'm not going to tell you what each signal means as far as my team is concerned because my manager would slaughter me, but it's for you and your manager to work out your own signals.

So what sort of corners can there be? Well, there's the long corner beyond the far post, the corner to the far post, the corner to the near post, the short corner, the corner to the middle of the edge of the penalty area, the corner plumb into the middle of the area, the floating corner, the corner that's whipped in violently looking for a touch or a ricochet, the outswinging corner, the inswinging corner, etc, etc. I don't mean to go on, but merely to underline just how many options you've got from a corner kick and just how important it is for you to try and win corners. Rather than penalty shoot outs, I'm a great believer in deciding drawn matches by the number of corners won, it shows a team has been attacking and it would encourage teams to attack. It would also mean goalies would try and hold on to saves rather than touching them around the post or over the cross-bar, which means they'd make more mistakes, which means more goals. Any way you look at it, it'd be more exciting for 90 minutes and much fairer than the penalty nightmares we had to go through in the World Cup.

You have to remember when you're taking the corner that your side is outnumbered because you're effectively out of the game. However, you have to overcome that by movement off the ball before the corner's taken, trying to drag the defence out of position, either by someone in your team making a dummy early run or even just by moving backwards and forwards or around in a circle. It's amazing how distracting that can be for a defence. You always have to remember to play to the strength of your team. If your forward line is six inches shorter than the opposition defence then the high ball to the far post is more likely to be headed out than headed in. In those circumstances the short corner, or a low hard corner, will be more effective. Assuming you're not a team of midgets playing a team of giants then you'll probably favour the high, long outswinging corner, just out of the keeper's reach to the far post, where your attacker will climb either for a direct header or a knock back across the face of the goal. I've illustrated that below.

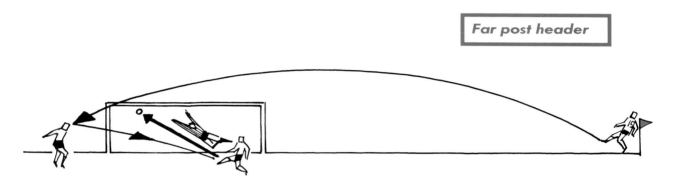

Far post header

There's nothing very sophisticated about that, but it's worked to great effect for the likes of Millwall and Wimbledon who have had big strikers and good headers at times in the shapes of Cascarino and Sheringham, Fashanu and Cork. As you'll see, the knock back makes defenders turn back on themselves, as, having followed the flight of the ball to the attacker, they find it's put behind them when it's played back across.

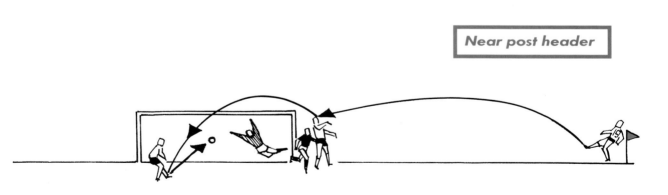

Near post header

The complete opposite of the far post header is the short corner which is most effective when played as a 1–2. That pulls defenders out of the box towards the ball, but if you play it quickly enough still gives you time to get a better angle for your cross, with enough space to get weight on it.

Even if you don't play a 1–2, if your team mate breaks away from the penalty box quickly enough and receives the ball in the right position he can make a more telling contribution with his cross than you could with your corner.

I've already mentioned Clive Allen, and nobody scored more goals from corners at the near post than he did for Spurs. Near post goal scoring, whether it's from crosses or corners, is a real art form and one that not many players have actually conquered. It's something you really have to work on, the angle is usually difficult and the ball is going to come at you very fast.

TURN ANKLE SLIGHTLY FOR SIDE FOOT GLANCE

Side foot shot or side foot glance to opposite corner

If you're aiming at near post headers you've got to be sure not to put the ball too near the keeper otherwise he'll snaffle it up. Ideally, you want to give your team mate either the chance of a knock on with the head or else a flick in with the head or foot like Clive Allen.

As a variation, try hitting it low and hard, or else low and at an angle beyond the near post huddle. That'll give your attackers the chance to run in and score.

As you've probably gathered by now this book is more about attack than

Power hit low corner. Ball hit with instep

defence, but obviously if your team is defending they ought to be close marking – on a man to man basis – all the attackers. As I said before, you as a defending team have got one more man than they have so it shouldn't be difficult. However, you should have two defenders actually on the goal line, usually one inside each post, covering up in case the keeper's beaten. The question is whether or not those defenders can mark an attacker while also doing their clearance duties – difficult decision isn't it? The one thing you have to be sure of is not to give a big attacker a free header because if you do and he's any good he's very likely to score.

Taking the move one step further, once the ball is played back outside the box then many defences fancy the offside trap. However, that's really a military exercise and if you can't do it properly then don't do it at all. With the new offside rule coming in to play, i.e. you're not offside if you're level with the last man, it's even more difficult to achieve.

The corner I really fancy is the one I whip in as an inswinger. Again you have to get the ball to come in beyond the keeper's reach so the weight and timing on the ball have to be perfect. I've shown on the next page just how to do it, but don't do it every time otherwise it has no element of surprise.

If you're a little person and you're reading this (or even littler and having it read to you) you may have a problem in getting a corner to reach the penalty area let alone the far post. In order to practise and build up the strength in your kicking foot, take the corners from half way between the goal and the corner flag, then gradually move back, day by day, week by week, until you find that you can get the ball the whole way across.

What you have to remember is that for the person taking a corner, it is just another kind of pass, but for that pass not to be wasted his team mates have to know what he's going to do with it. The only way to know that is to practise, practise, practise. Remember to lean back, and remember that the quicker you bring up your knee the quicker the ball will go up and come down. For more height, lean further back, but to whip it in just skip off the left standing foot. Try not to take a long run up. That, in itself, can give away the kind of corner you're going to take. I always reckon that if you take three steps, then after the first step, even before you've touched the ball, a good defence will be attacking the corner kick.

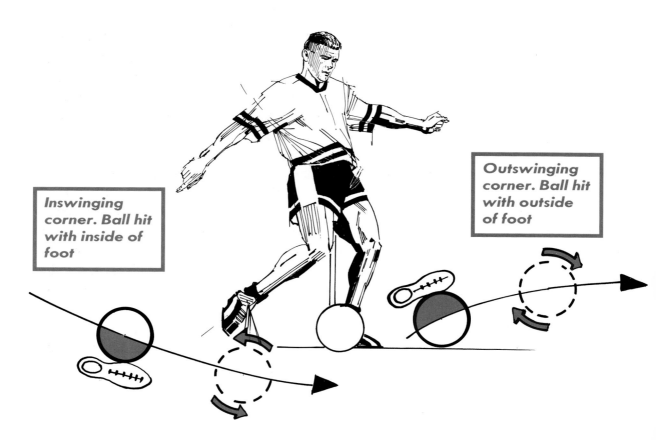

Inswinging corner. Ball hit with inside of foot

Outswinging corner. Ball hit with outside of foot

Instep power drive

Placed side foot shot

Another thing to practise is penalties, even if you're not the penalty taker. Everybody in the team should be able to take a penalty if he has to. At the level that most young readers play, penalty shoot outs are unlikely, but the first prize I ever won in the game was for a schools penalty competition. Until I win a World Cup Winner's medal it's the trophy I'll treasure the most. I remember dashing home with it to show my mum and dad and taking it to bed with me in case it vanished overnight.

When you're a goalkeeper and you're standing on your own between the posts the goal looks immense. When you're the penalty taker it's the goalie who looks big, almost like he's filling the whole of the goal mouth. It's better not to look at him. There's no worse time to have eye contact with the goalie than when you're taking a penalty. Keep your eye on the ball, and that'll help you keep your head down anyway. If your head is down, you've more chance of keeping your body over the ball which means you've less chance of blasting it over the bar.

You've really two choices with a penalty; blasting it or placing it. If you blast accurately, then even if the keeper gets to it, provided his body's not behind the ball, it should go in. If you're going to go for height, then try and keep the ball low (just try telling Chris Waddle about that!).

If you're going to place the ball, aim for the corners and try and disguise the direction. Mick Quinn of Newcastle has an unusual approach to penalty taking. He stands with his back to the keeper, almost challenging the defenders to encroach into the area. He then turns suddenly, takes three steps, and hits the ball nice and low.

Whatever you do, don't look at the keeper and don't wait for him to move. Most referees nowadays seem to give the keeper the benefit of the doubt in those situations and you should be concentrating on scoring first time rather than giving yourself the chance of taking the penalty again.

Again, practise penalties on your own, either with an empty goal or else by hitting chalked numbers on a wall. If you can then imagine when you take your penalty in a real match that the keeper's not there, you're half way to scoring. One of the most successful penalty takers in the League (I won't give his name in case he thinks I'm giving away secrets) takes a fair run at the ball, five or six paces. He has a good look at the goalkeeper's legs. If the keeper moves he blasts it; if he keeps still throughout the run up, then he places it.

I've already shown in the drawings how you should hit a power penalty and how to place one. Don't try and copy the flick with the back of my heel I sometimes try in friendlies. It gives me and the crowd a lot of fun, but I don't think your coach will be too pleased if you fall flat on your face while trying to take a penalty!

Surprise penalty shot crossing one leg behind the other

BALANCE AND THE USE OF THE BODY · 13

I've already talked about control, and in this chapter I'm talking not just about controlling the ball but controlling your body. Unless you've eyes in the back of your head, for the most part you'll receive the ball facing the opposite direction from where you want to go. You have to be able to control the ball and get your body and feet round the right way, often with an opponent hustling you at the same time. I'm not worried here about what the opposition's doing, or even what you can or can't do against the opponent. Before you can get up to any clever stuff, you've first got to be able to receive and turn.

If the ball's coming to you, you have to be into your turn almost before you receive it. Your weight goes on to the non-kicking foot. Feel balanced. If you're not balanced it won't work, just as you have to be perfectly balanced before you set off on a run. It's like riding a bike, if you wobble along for a few yards you're probably going to fall off.

Receive the ball with your kicking foot and take the pace off it with the inside of your foot (there you are, that's a trapping skill put into practice). Be relaxed, be balanced and keep your eye on the ball. Don't be distracted, either by a player coming in on you, or by yelling and shouting around you. In one movement take the ball around, turning on your non-kicking foot. Then switch the ball from one foot to another, at the same time switching your weight.

Shielding the ball and turning

Now you'll rarely have time to do it exactly that way in a game because you can't wait for the ball to come to you, but practise it like that for a while. Either throw the ball against a wall yourself, trap, control and turn, or else play with a friend, passing to each other, with the receiver completing a whole turn and then returning the ball with the opposite foot, the one with which he received it. No harm in ringing the changes – it gives you the chance to practise using both feet.

Right: Shielding the ball. Arm held away from the body

Cruyff turn at speed

1

BRAKE

2

FLICK BALL BACK AND TURN

Now that you feel comfortable on the turn (well you do, don't you?) you can work on turning defenders. Sometimes I like to turn a defender twice. Ask me why. Go on. All right, be like that – I'll tell you anyway. It's because one good turn deserves another – as the two bottles of sour milk said to each other. Enough of this, concentrate Gazza, concentrate reader.

A lot's been written about a turn I did against Holland in the World Cup which is known as the 'Cruyff turn'. It's really a question of dragging the ball behind your left foot with your right, after dummying to go the other way.

Turning involves all the skills I've already mentioned, touch, feel, instant control and most of all balance and disguise. The obvious turn and the one that's most easily intercepted is taking the ball with your right foot (where it's your natural foot) and moving in a semi-circle to your left. It's easy to read, slow to do, and leaves daylight for a fair tackle from behind.

I'm not saying don't ever do it, but don't do it all the time. Keep springing surprises and keep the defenders on their toes.

If you turn with the outside of your foot then provided another defender's not covering the defender covering you, you've a much better chance of getting away with it. If you dip your left shoulder and put a bit of weight on your left foot the defender will think you're going left, having taken the ball on the inside of your right foot. What you do is take it on the outside of the right foot and go right. The defender's off balance, you're on balance and you're away.

You can reverse this by pretending to go for a turn on the outside and then suddenly turning in *towards* the defender and then going past him on the inside (unless and until he takes you from behind). Believe me, all the skill players in the game really welcome the sending off for a 'professional' foul. There's nothing worse than turning your defender perfectly, being balanced just right, heading off for goal and being brought down. It's not good for you, it's not good for the game and it's not good for the spectators.

I've included a couple more little turns on the next page and later on when talking about special tricks. It's a bit of the game the crowd enjoy seeing, so 'turn it on for them'!

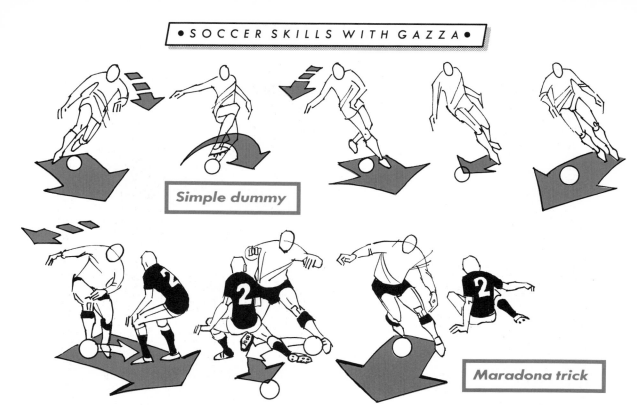

Simple dummy

Maradona trick

I've mentioned 'dummies' and 'dropping your shoulder' in passing and nobody does this better than my old mate Chris Waddle. (He won't like the old, but when you're past 30 and still have the worst haircut in European football what do you expect?)

A dummy is simply a term for pretending to do one thing and then doing another. A perfect dummy is done when you're perfectly balanced, a bit like a plane tilting in flight.

Dummying on the ball also looks good when it's properly done but you must have worked on it in practice otherwise your team mates can be fooled too. Try and take a defender out of the game with your dummy. A classical dummy is when the ball is played from midfield into the first striker at the edge of the box. The second striker will call 'over'. The first striker then lets the ball through his legs to travel to the second striker. The first striker then spins and faces up ready to receive the ball back. He's lost his marker and is ready to go for goal.

A less glamorous use of your body is to screen the ball. You often see a team with a narrow lead haring off to the corner with the ball in the dying seconds of a match. The player with the ball faces the crowd, his back to the goal and the defender has somehow to get in a tackle past his body. Often the defender gives away a foul, a corner or a throw in, all of which waste more valuable seconds.

Chris Waddle on a run, dropping his shoulder

That's a negative part of the game which I don't like, but shielding can be necessary to buy yourself a bit of time until there's something on for you to do with the ball. At the same time as you shield the ball with your body there's nothing illegal in holding out your arms slightly behind your body. It helps your balance, it makes you more awkward to tackle and it tells you exactly where your opponent is.

You have to draw a line between legal shielding and illegal backing in. It's difficult for the referee to tell the two apart, but provided you keep the ball as far in front of you as possible with your kicking foot and bend your knees a little, it'll be hard for the ref to make a decision against you. The further the ball is away from the guy coming up your rear, the more likely it is he'll do something silly and give away a free kick.

You can't stay with your body between the ball and the opponent forever, so either lay the ball back, or try and half turn to get sideways on, playing the ball with the outside of your kicking foot – and then lay the ball off whenever you've got the room. A pass is usually better than a turn when you've been screening because the defender will be so close to you that the turn will be difficult, if not a bit obvious. However, you never know ... a drop of the shoulder, a dummy, a shimmy, and away you go – at least that's how it always happens in 'Roy of the Rovers'.

DRIBBLING AND RUNNING WITH THE BALL ·14

In order to dribble properly, the one thing you need more than anything else is confidence. If you feel you can go forward with the ball, if you feel you can take people on, then do it. It's the most exciting thing to watch in the game – a player on a run, going past players with pace and swerve, hurdling tackles. If you think you've a better path to goal than anybody else, then go for it. If you haven't then lay it off, but only if your team mates have moved up with you and are in a better position than you are. There's no point in beating five players and then passing to someone who's tightly marked. He's certain to lose it, and when he does, you look great and he looks a wally. That's not what dribbling's about and it's not fair on your team mates nor will it make you popular with them.

There's an element of the body swerve in a good dribbling run, an element of balance, there's ball control and maybe the drop of the shoulder and the dummy, but what you also need to be able to do is change your pace. My Newcastle team mate Mirandinha had electrifying speed, but that was it. He set off fast, he ran fast and he finished fast; what I think is more effective is ringing the changes in pace.

> **Shielding the ball. Arm held away from the body**

Sometimes when I'm running with the ball I feel as if I've got different gears (no, not a change of clothing – I mean like a car). There's a power gear to get up speed, and then a cruising gear when you've reached top speed. The art is to run like you're an automatic car with each gear going smoothly into place without a clunk of the clutch; but the brakes are just as important. If you stop suddenly during a run you can throw the defence off balance, particularly if you set off again immediately. You can make to pass during your run, then carry on, but whatever you do keep going forward. If you run at the defence you've a chance of opening them up. Try not to get pushed wide, since, if you do, you're probably running into a blind alley. If you keep going, beating man after man, they're out of the game and each time somebody else has to come across and cover, freeing one of your team mates when you decide it's the right time to pass.

Reverse turn

FOOT ON BALL, DRAG BACK

Don't just use one foot on a run if you can help it, or if you do, use both the inside and outside of the foot. It gives you pace and variety and keeps the opposition guessing.

You've tried working with cones, but cones don't try and tackle you. So now try an exercise which is effectively one and one with you trying to beat the man (or boy), (or toddler – or if you're very young, the twinkle in your dad's eye) on the inside and the outside.

Don't throw your cones away. Try a race in and out of them. If you go fast enough you can almost believe they're trying to tackle you.

We'll deal with tackling next, but assuming the team you're playing read this book back to front they'll know how to tackle which means you should know how to ride one. One good way is to push the ball just that little bit ahead of you, not so far as to lose control, but just enough to make the defender expect you to arrive a split second before you actually do. You hurdle his leg, meet up with the ball and he's left sprawling. As Del Boy would say, 'lovely jubbly!'

Gazza shows the dip of the shoulder and the famous swerve against the old enemy

Gazza running with the ball

So, combine pace with balance, a swerve of the body, a dip of the shoulder, and you'll be on your way, although sometimes a bad defender has a better chance of stopping your feint or swerve than a good one, simply because he won't see it coming. What you should be prepared to do then is to make your dummy or feint your real action – if you see the defender's not buying it, then go through with it. That really takes skill, balance and quick thinking. You may not be top of your class at school work (there was never any chance of me getting to that position either) but if you can see that move through there's no way you can be called thick.

Here's one more exercise from the 30 yard line. Have the keeper on the line, with one defender just inside the area, and another defender a few yards in front of him. Take the ball on the outside of your foot and run at the first defender, feint one way, but go on the outside of him, then feint the other way and go inside the second defender. End up with a shot at the keeper, who'll be coming off the line and spreading his body. This also teaches you how to draw the keeper. Then try it with one of the defenders turning and pursuing you. He's allowed to put in another tackle (he's not allowed to chop you down!).

You can also try dribbling on your own. Keep your head up. Don't look at the ball. You'll soon know where it is instinctively. Then try dribbling with loads of kids around you. Keep control of your ball and avoid bumping into any of the other kids. This teaches control, balance and awareness.

The thing to do on a run is not to have it all planned out in your mind; be aware of the options open to you and adapt, depending upon what your opponent does, and also upon what your own team mates are doing. The best run ends either with a goal or else what I said when Magnus Magnusson asked me my name in Mastermind ... pass!

Gazza keeps his balance and leaves his Cameroon opponent sprawling

Left: It's all about balance. The Dutch are left panting yards behind as Gazza strokes the ball away with his right foot
Below: This time it's Gazza's left about to do the damage. He's perfectly positioned and balanced which is more than can be said for his opponents

TACKLING · 15

What's that you said, the nearest Gazza gets to tackle is in a fishing shop! Not true. I reckon tackling's a strong part of my game. It has to be when you play in midfield. You've got to stop the opposition midfield coming forward, from linking up with their strikers. Me, I like chess. Funnily enough I reckon it's the board game that comes nearest to football. The goal's the King, and you've got to defend it to the death, but if you don't attack with the likes of your rooks down the flank you can't make progress in the middle with your knights and bishops. I won't say the Queen's the playmaker as otherwise every playmaker in the country will sue me for libel, but it really is that way.

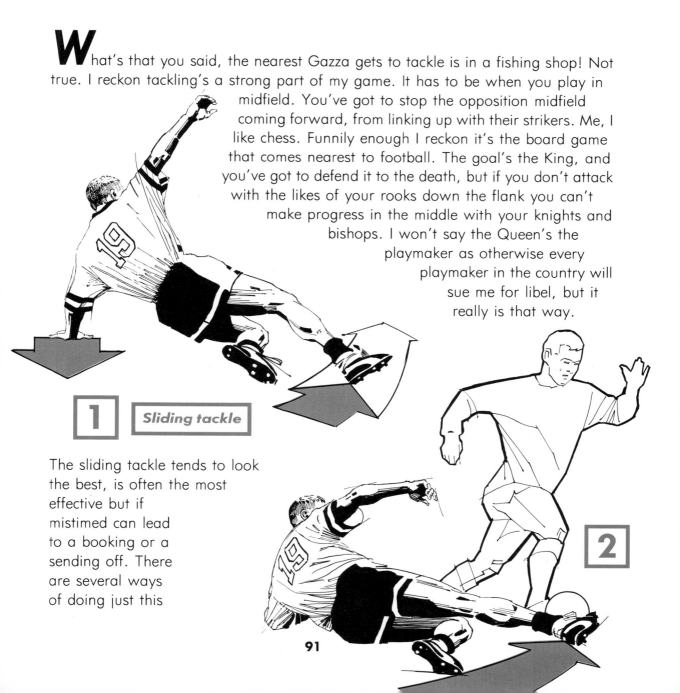

1 Sliding tackle

The sliding tackle tends to look the best, is often the most effective but if mistimed can lead to a booking or a sending off. There are several ways of doing just this

2

one tackle. You can go in with the outside of the foot, with your other leg to the side of the body and try and hook around to win the ball.

Or you can go in with the sole of the foot, with your other leg *under* the body.

Am I boring you? I'm not ... good, then I'll carry on. Try this one, trapping the ball with the inside of the foot but sideways.

Or what about ringing the changes and trapping the ball with the inside of the foot with the other leg bent under the body, or trying to kick the ball away to your team mate rather than trapping. Whatever you do don't commit yourself to a tackle too early. Make sure you are ready; if necessary close your opponent down before you go in for the kill (I don't mean that literally, honest ref!). By doing that you'll have a chance of 'jockeying' him into a worse position, and giving your team mates time to cut off his alternatives (very painful that, I'm told).

Whichever kind of tackle you choose keep your eye on the ball and try and force your opponent into the first move, let him commit himself before you do. (Actually quite a few of my team mates have said I should be committed, do you think that's what they meant?)

The other most effective kind of tackle is a block tackle which you make facing your opponent (the sliding tackle is usually from the side, or slightly behind the opponent).

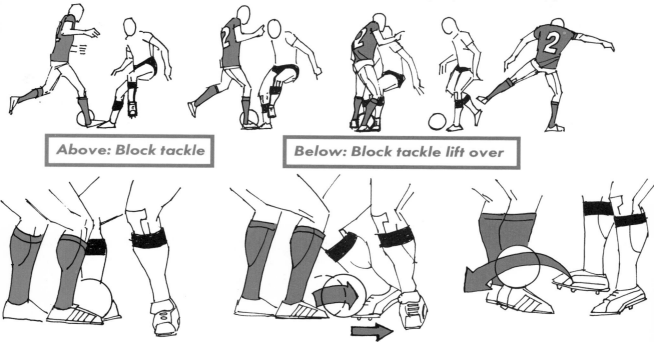

Above: Block tackle

Below: Block tackle lift over

BLOCK THE BALL   RELEASE FOOT SLIGHTLY   LIFT BALL OVER

More the Roeder run than the Roeder shuffle although Newcastle ended up on the losing side against Spurs in the Cup in February 1987

This you do with the inside of your foot and the weight of your body behind the ball and obviously behind the tackling foot. Always stand up nice and straight, keep yourself solid. There's going to be a crunch but if you pull away at the last minute you stand more chance of getting hurt than if you go right through with it. The same is true if you go in half-heartedly.

Try and come out of the tackle with a bit of style and panache. There's no point in winning the ball, dwelling on it smugly, and then losing it as someone comes in and pounces on you. One technique I rather like, although we used to take the mickey out of it at Newcastle, is the Roeder shuffle. I could just have easily included that in the

The Roeder shuffle

section on dribbling but somehow it seems more in place here as Glen would use it to great effect after he'd won the ball in a tackle and was moving forward. It had the effect of disorientating the midfield or defenders who were facing him and I've never understood why more players didn't adopt it as a tactic.

Try playing the alley game. Make yourself an alley between two lines of half cones. Have a goal of cones at either end. You have to beat your opponent, keep within the alley, and then score between the cone-goals. Keep score up to ten and then change ends. The good defence will force the attacker wide (or in this case out of the alley) and then you have to hand over the ball to your opponent.

Alley game

THROW-INS • 16

WRONG

RIGHT

THUMBS BEHIND BALL

The worst sin any player can commit in the game is to do a foul throw and give away possession to the opposition. All you have to remember is that both feet have to be on the ground when the ball leaves both your hands, both feet have to be behind the line, and your arms have to come from behind your head and go over your head. Easy isn't it. Yet even when it's not a foul throw, it's often a lousy one.

Most teams now have their throw-in expert, one who brings something a little different to the game. Malcolm Macdonald (that man again) is the first I can remember who could turn a throw-in into a corner kick. He could get the ball right into the penalty area using the strength of his trunk and the windmill effect of his arms. I think it was the carry through of the throw that gave him the length and the height.

The Republic of Ireland have got Mick McCarthy who does something very similar. Although I was sitting on the bench I could not help noticing (and hearing) how excited the crowd got in the European qualifier against England at Lansdowne Road in Dublin every time the home team had a throw-in.

I ought to mention that you shouldn't take the throw-in just for the sake of getting rid of the ball. Even if the crowd's howling its impatience, you take your time, pick your man and then throw. A simple throw is to a team mate who chests it down, turns his man and then lays it off. There you are, three skills we've learned – I hope.

BALL BEHIND
BACK OF
HEAD

ARCH BACK

Another throw is to a player facing you for him to knock on with his head – the backward flicked header.

Very effective can be the throw down the line. That means exactly what it says, down the touchline for one of your players to run on to and hopefully cross. At worst

you'll gain ground, a bit like rugby, by gaining another throw, because the defenders will find it difficult to keep the ball in play. Use that throw defensively, especially in your own half. The throw has to be right down the line, not on the inside. Even professionals practise getting that just right.

Only take the throw quickly when there's something on for one of your team mates and there's movement off the ball. That way you've a good chance of catching the opposition unprepared – just make sure your team mate's not unprepared as well! Don't try and gain ground by inching along the touchline with the ball in your hands.

Short throw

96

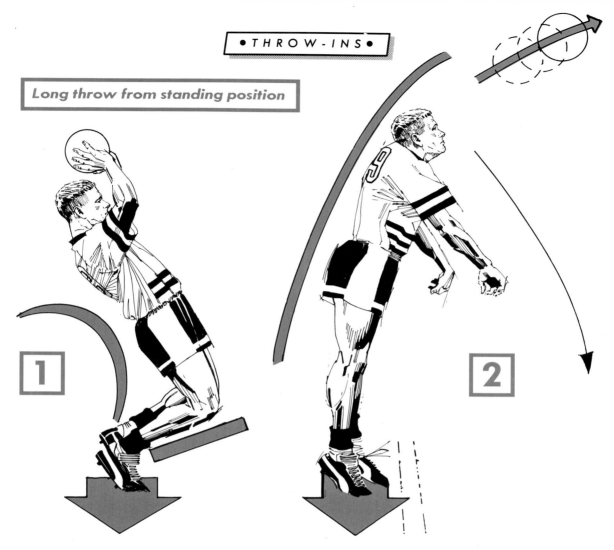

Long throw from standing position

1

2

Referees aren't stupid. They'll either send you back if they're nice guys or give the throw the other way if they're not.

One throw-in that's getting a lot of attention is the one by young Stephen Watson at Newcastle, who starts with a somersault to give himself velocity. No, it's not a foul throw, his feet are on the ground when he lets go of the ball.

I'm showing you the two alternative positions for throw-ins. For the short one, the knees will be bent, with the body forward, for the long throw the player's on tiptoe stretching to height and distance rather than power and velocity.

I like the story of the bloke who always took a ruler out after a throw. Eventually his team mates asked him why. 'Well, I've just thrown it in for good measure,' he replied!

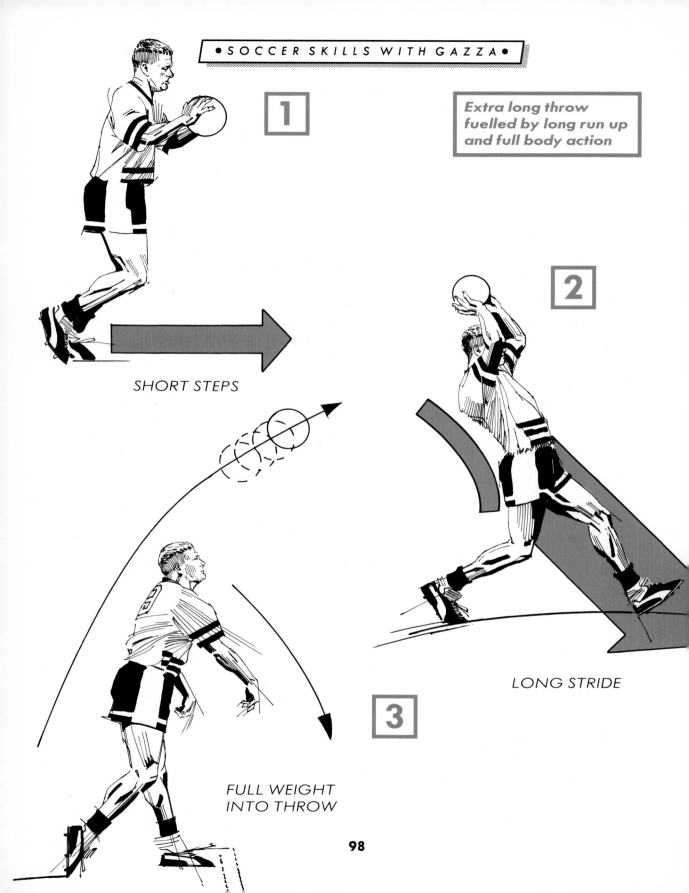

• SOCCER SKILLS WITH GAZZA •

1

Extra long throw fuelled by long run up and full body action

SHORT STEPS

2

LONG STRIDE

3

FULL WEIGHT INTO THROW

RUNNING OFF THE BALL ·17

*T*his is something you can't really practise on your own. Well, you can, but you'll look really silly running around without the ball; yet the interesting statistic (I hate people who start conversations with: 'Did you know ... ?' Normally I don't know, and the reason I don't is because I didn't want to) is that you spend a lot more time on the pitch without the ball than with it. That doesn't mean you should just fade out of the game. Obviously in midfield there's a lot less room to hide than in some other places on the pitch, but just because you're not involved in move after move doesn't mean that you're not playing your part. Making a run off the ball can be just as important as dribbling, because you're probably taking one of the opposition with you, and maybe at the same time giving the player with the ball an option of passing to you if you're not too heavily marked. You have to offer yourself (not literally) to your team mates, making sure they know that you're there. Running off the ball is the final proof that football's a team game.

WRONG

No angle for pass

RIGHT

Angle for pass

WRONG

No angle to pass

RIGHT

Dummy run creates space for pass

The 'decoy' run is intended to draw opposition players out of position and to confuse them. You're never going to get the ball, you know that, your team mate with the ball knows that, but the opposition don't. When you pull away you must look as if you're ready to receive the ball. If you take a defender with you, then you've created space for your man to move into.

If the defender doesn't go with you, then if your team mate's quick he should try and turn your decoy run into a real run and pass to you.

In training try and practise moving and running off the ball by playing the midfield and forwards against the back four, starting from the half way line and heading for goal. Your coach should stop and organise you as you move forward, showing you where he wants you to go (and doubtless explaining quietly and politely where you've gone wrong).

Try improvising a game of shadow football. Play without opposition, building up from the goalkeeper. Restrict the number of touches each player can have, focus on movement and support – the support coming from running off the ball. Then have a go at hitting one of your target men with the other one moving into decoy positions.

Although he was a bit before my time, Martin Peters, I'm told, was one of the best exponents (big word that!) of 'ghosting' into positions. This means getting into a vital position, either to receive the ball, or score a goal, without the defence realising what you are doing. To do this most effectively you have to ignore the ball – which sounds a bit odd when it's the only piece of playing equipment on the field apart from the goal posts. However you'll find that most players do concentrate on the ball. Consequently if the ball is, say, on the left wing, you should ghost in on the right, behind the defence, or as we say on their 'blind side'. You have to time it dead right. If you get there too early, the defender will become aware of you – maybe he'll turn, maybe the keeper will yell out and draw you to his attention. If you get there too late the keeper will come off his line and snaffle the ball up.

Provided you've lost your defender when the cross field pass comes, you should be left with a free shot or a free header.

Diagonal pass directed into the path of a blind side run

When you ghost in don't call out for the ball. Ghosts don't speak. However, you can raise your arm to try and attract the attention of your team mate with the ball (or else rattle some bones).

The overlapping full back is another vital 'support player' in the modern game whose selfless running often draws the attention of the opposition when the ball is played away from him either inside or across the field. He really has to be superfit because having galloped half way down the pitch and not got the ball, he has to dash back in readiness to defend. The run will however give the man on the ball some choices, either to play the ball down the line to the overlapping player, or to use him as a decoy.

It can get a bit frustrating to keep making these runs and not get the ball. Crowds tend to watch the players on the ball rather than those off it. However, your team mates will appreciate selfless running. Paul Stewart and Gary Lineker often run miles in a match without receiving a ball – but that doesn't mean they're not playing an effective part for their team. Football's not just about passing and scoring, it's also about hard running and hard work, it's a team game and the glory boys couldn't get the glory without the workers.

Here is the start of the Beardsley trick...

...going well...

...the final move, selling the perfect dummy. The opponent (or Nicky in this case) is left off balance and Gazza's away

DRAWING THE KEEPER, ACCELERATION, GOAL POACHING ·18

Drawing the keeper is a real art form (drawing, art, get it?). The object of the exercise is to tempt the keeper off his line with a view to chipping him or hitting the ball outside of his reach by swerving it past him.

The keeper's main concern is to narrow the angle, spread his body, and reduce the target you have to aim at. He's going to try and force you wide, by spreading himself, but one thing you have to remember is that most keepers come out low. It's

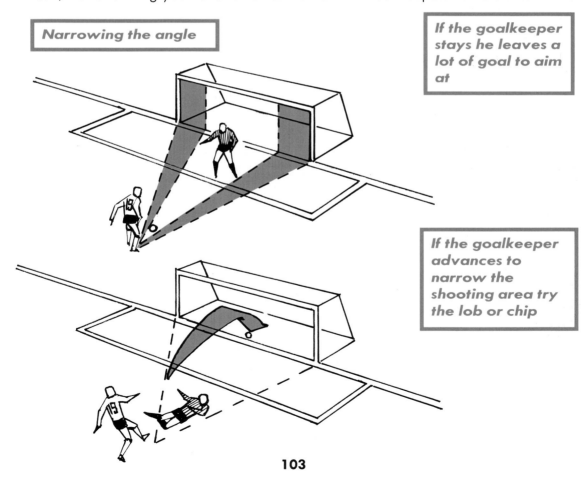

Narrowing the angle

If the goalkeeper stays he leaves a lot of goal to aim at

If the goalkeeper advances to narrow the shooting area try the lob or chip

tempting to try and blast the ball, but if you keep your head all you need to do is lift the ball over the keeper (not over the bar please) and into the net. Kenny Dalglish was a real master of that. I remember a goal he scored for Liverpool against Bruges in the Eurpoean Cup Final. The object is a delicate chip rather than a power blast. Draw your foot back, and try and fool the keeper into thinking you're going to wellie it, then pull the shot back, get your toes under the ball and chip it. Peter Beardsley also does that to perfection.

If you see the keeper is a bit slow in getting down then try and slip the ball through the gap between his body and the ground.

The keeper is going to try and make you make the first move. You try and get him to commit himself, but remember time is of the essence in the penalty box. If you delay too long the keeper will be off his line and on top of you before you realise it, or alternatively a defender will have time to get across and cover with a sideways on tackle or a sliding tackle.

Some keepers will try and read your eyes, so as I've said before don't look where you're going to put the ball. Try and stare the keeper in the eyes and flick the ball past him. Don't run the ball too far ahead of you – if you show too much of it to the keeper, he'll attack the ball and dispossess you. You should be the one doing the attacking, not allowing yourself to be attacked.

In your approach work to goal, acceleration and pace can be vital. Try and get the keeper (or the defence) off balance as you approach by changing pace. If a defender gets near you, stop suddenly, turn him and then try and accelerate again. Working the close space of the penalty area, try and get the opposition, and particularly the keeper, unsettled by not making a straight run at goal at a steady speed, but whatever you do keep on the move. Once you stop with the ball, or once the keeper succeeds in stopping you, then the odds are on the keeper making the save.

Even if you've completed your run, hang around for a rebound. It's called goal poaching but there's nothing illegal about it. Remember the dangers of being offside. Too many teams at all levels of the game play the offside trap nowadays. If you concentrate you shouldn't be caught offside – it's just plain careless and lazy not to look along the line.

ANALYSING THE OPPOSITION AND ANALYSING YOUR OWN TEAM

·19

I said earlier in the book that you shouldn't worry too much about the opposition; but on the other hand you should know what you're up against and take the appropriate steps. If your opponents have a full back who's too eager to get forward then your wingers should be ready and willing to get in behind him. If the opposition score a lot of goals from set pieces, work on those moves in training; be ready but don't be afraid.

As far as your own team is concerned, each player, each position, has its own particular requirements. Your keeper should be fairly tall. You get good short keepers, but you don't get great ones. He needs good safe hands, mobility and fine reflexes. Catching is all important. If he gets the ball he should be able to catch it and stop it bouncing back into play with a chance of your opponent poaching a goal. When we filmed 'Gazza's Soccer School' at Wembley recently we came across a fine young goalkeeper in the shape of Andrew Quy who was only fourteen and was actually catching my best shot, coming off his line really fast and spreading his body like a seasoned professional.

Andrew Quy in goalmouth action. Yes, he did save it

Then there are the full backs. They should have the ability to get forward, to play as support wingers, and they need a bit of pace to counter fast raiding attackers. If your team is playing a sweeper system then the full backs should be able to get even further forward to start and create attacks. However they also need to be able to tackle back at speed or else they'll give away free kicks in vital positions.

If you play a sweeper, his prime ability must be awareness of what's going on around him. There's a strong argument for always playing an experienced player as a sweeper, but I'm a great believer in the saying that if you're good enough you're old enough. Paul Parker of QPR and England is a good example of that. There's no doubt though, that the sweeper role is good for captaincy because of the vision of the whole game you get. Captain or not, the sweeper needs the respect of the whole team because they have to allow themselves to be organised by him.

The central defence, surprise surprise, needs defence-minded players. They should have height and pace with the ability to tackle. They also must be prepared to go forward for set pieces and corners with enough pace to get back in case defence turns into attack.

The midfield needs balance. Two similar players don't usually slot in comfortably side by side. The midfield must be able to organise and tackle, to win the ball and spread it around, all with a touch of flair as well as efficiency. If one of the midfielders is tempted to move too far forward, the others must be prepared to come in and fill the gap. I think you're also looking for width from the midfield, particularly when a team doesn't play traditional orthodox wingers. They must be able to take a man on, beat him and then put in accurate crosses.

With two up front in a 4–4–2 formation they must also complement and balance each other. I've always wanted to see Gary Lineker and Ian Rush play in the same side as I feel they'd complement each other ideally with their hard work on and off the ball, their ability and willingness to chase and hurry and their clinical accurate finishing. Alternatively the system works with a tough direct striker and a skilful ball player. Less imaginative, but often effective, is a big receiver, good in the air, able to knock down the ball for his fast running partner. The best of strikers work in pairs. Bannister and Warboys – the smash and grab of Bristol Rovers in the 1970s, Macdonald and Tudor of Newcastle of the same era, Bull and Mutch at Wolves, Lineker and Stewart or Walsh at Spurs, or Lineker and Beardsley who were so successful for so long in the English team.

Ian Rush, master striker, just look at his stance, nice and upright, the outstep of his boot perfectly positioned for running with the ball

The best of strikers hunt in pairs, but what about Malcolm Macdonald's hairstyle...

Across the board you're looking for variety and balance. You can't play with eleven sprinters, eleven giants or eleven sweepers. What you have to be sure of is that you do play with eleven triers.

SPECIAL TRICKS • 20

I've already mentioned the Cruyff turn, but here at the end of the book (do I hear sighs of relief, muffled cheers?) is a good place to try it again. Dummy as if you're going to pass or cross then draw the ball back with the inside of your foot behind you, wait for your opponent to go off balance, complete your turn and move away with either your left foot or the outside of your right foot.

Cruyff turn

While we're on the subject of named players, there's my Beardsley trick. Show your opponent the inside of the foot, then twist your body and play it with the outside of the other foot while the opponent is off balance, like the photographs on page 102.

Beardsley trick

As you've probably gathered, Chris Waddle is one of my favourite players as well as one of my best friends. Mind you, he did leave Newcastle to get away from me and then when I followed him to Tottenham he remembered my fear of flying and actually went abroad leaving me behind. I like his feint to the right, a drop of the right shoulder, step over the ball with your left foot and then bring it away with the outside of the right foot.

Waddle move

You can actually vary that by reversing the process.

A trick that relies on change of pace is to stop and start, pushing the ball forward then stopping it with your right foot while quickly playing the ball with your left foot coming through from behind. That has to be done all in one swift movement.

Dummy back heel

Again for a change you can dummy over the ball letting it run on with its own velocity whilst pretending to back heel.

Rocastle trick

Then just to show I'm not biased, there's the David Rocastle trick. As the ball is moving step over it with your right foot, then step over it with your left. As the opponent is off balance take it away with the outside of your right foot.

Then there's Steve Coppell (no I'm not asking for a transfer to Crystal Palace). You drop your left shoulder here and then whilst at an angle push your body out to the right and, using the outside of your right foot, push the ball away from the opponent.

Coppell trick

Finally just dummy over the ball with one foot and come back with the other foot ready to play it. Sounds terribly simple but it's enough to put your opponent off balance and sometimes the simplest tricks can be the best.

A couple of fun non-playing tricks are to pretend to throw the ball down in temper and then just to block it as it hits your toes. That usually gets a good laugh and can defuse a heated situation. Make sure you smile when you do it.

I also like to pretend not to be able to pick the ball up. Reach forward for it and then bring your foot up and kick it forward, keep repeating the process until everybody's sick and tired of it!

So there you have it. There's no way I've been able to go through everything in this book. Even as I get to this stage I can think of all sorts of things I've not touched on, such as making a wall, marking your man, squeezing your orange at half time ... However, I hope that I've dealt with enough to make you not only a better player but also to make you want to practise to be a better player. So keep at it, keep trying, keep competing. I'll be watching you and who knows, one day I may be playing with you, or against you. You're the future of the game, you're tomorrow's hero, you're the threat to my position. Maybe I shouldn't have written this book after all ...